TABLE OF CONTENTS

Preface

This book is a step-by-step introduction to financial accounting fundamentals. It is designed for persons who use financial statements, documents that summarize results of the accounting process. Consequently, informed financial statement analysis requires an understanding of accounting.

Financial statements

The accounting system provides for recording financial information, classifying this information, and developing financial statements. People in business use these financial statements in their work and in managing personal investments. These financial statement users include investors when considering whether to buy, sell, or hold securities; lenders when evaluating loan requests; and suppliers when deciding whether to extend credit. Many business managers rank financial statements among their most important tools.

Why statement users need specific training

People sometimes ask why people in business should be trained to use financial statements. Given that the future analyst can read English, he or she might wonder about the need for specific training. One answer is that accounting is really a language. Accountants use vocabulary and conventions that are not obvious without specific orientation. Successful athletes know the rules of their games. Similarly, successful professionals in business know the accounting system.

Much of the book consists of examples and practice exercises. Specific terminology is less important than understanding procedures for developing financial statements and interpreting the income statement and balance sheet. Learning is by progression through a series of short but increasingly challenging exercises. Readers are advised to practice the concepts rather than try to memorize the material. The recommended approach is to review the text and numerical examples and then to work all exercises as a self-test. If you stumble on an exercise, review the earlier material and work the exercise again.

Chapter 1

Past performance and current status
(The income statement and balance sheet)

All financial statements include income statements and balance sheets. A major objective of this book is to make you comfortable with both documents. While working through this material, you will become very familiar with income statements and balance sheets and their relationship to cash flow.

Learning objectives

The objectives of this chapter include the following:

- To learn the exact meaning of revenues and expenses and how this knowledge assists in interpreting the income statement.
- To learn the exact meaning of assets, liabilities, and owners' equity and how to interpret the balance sheet.
- To understand how retained earnings are developed and how users should interpret this disclosure.
- To work with the balance sheet equation and see how this helps in evaluating financial statements.
- To learn the money measurement principle.

The income statement

Income measures financial performance. It addresses the question of How well did we do? Income is always measured over a prescribed period of time; this may be a month, a quarter, or a full year. Following is the income statement for Millennium Music Corporation, a store that sells records, tapes, and CDs:

Millennium Music Corporation
Income for the year ended December 31, 20x0

Sales Revenue		$240,000
Expenses		
Cost of Goods Sold	$90,000	
Other Expenses	80,000	170,000
Income		$ 70,000

Millennium Music's income statement begins with the name of the business and the period over which income is measured. In this case, income is for the full year ending December 31, 20x0. The statement shows three components common to all income statements: revenues, expenses, and income.

Revenues

Revenues are inflows to the business from providing services. Record shops and other retailers have sales revenue; advertising agencies have service revenues. Later we will see that revenues do not necessarily mean that cash is collected. For now, think of revenues simply as providing services.

Expenses

Expenses reflect the use of services. Millennium Music's income statement shows three categories of expenses. One is the Cost of Goods Sold. As the title suggests, this is simply the cost of the goods that were sold during the period. Other expenses include rent, salaries, and electricity usage. Now try the following exercises to be sure that you understand revenues and expenses.

Exercise 1-1

Revenues and Expenses. Professional Employment Agency, Inc. is preparing its income statement. One item is the cost of preparing and mailing advertising brochures. This would include word processing, printing, and mailing. Is the cost of preparing and mailing advertising brochures an expense?

Yes, the cost of preparing and mailing advertising brochures is an expense.

Solution

Yes, the cost of mailing is an expense. Word processing, printing, and mailing all entail the use of services.

Exercise 1-2

Revenues and Expenses. Three of the following items relate to revenues and three relate to expenses for Gloria's Garage, a gas station and repair business. Indicate R (for revenue) or E (for expense) as appropriate:

> *Tip: Does the transaction provide a service (revenue) or use a service (expense)?*

(R) E   The garage sells oil and gas.
R (E)   Gloria's Garage pays the rent.
(R) E   The business bills a customer $325 for car repairs.
(R) E   The garage earns $25 interest on its bank balance.
R (E)   Phone calls for the period cost $90.
R (E)   Property tax payments are $500.

Solution

The first, third, and fourth items are revenues for Gloria's Garage. The second, fifth, and sixth items are expenses. Remember that revenues mean providing services. When a service station provides gas, repairs cars, or earns interest on its bank deposits it has revenue. The business uses services when it rents space, makes phone calls, and pays taxes (for services provided by the government).

Income

Income is the difference between revenues and expenses. It measures financial performance. When revenues exceed expenses, the firm has income. Income is also called profit or earnings.

Exercise 1-3   **Income.** A portion of Whitestone Company's income statement for the year shows the following:

Whitestone Company
Income for the year ended December 31, 20x0

Sales Revenue		$1,800,000
Expenses		
Cost of Goods Sold	$1,200,000	
Rent Expense	300,000	
Salaries	50,000	1,550,000
Income		?

What is Whitestone's income?

$$1,800,000 - 1,550,000 = 250,000$$

Solution   The company's income is $250,000. This is the difference between revenues and expenses.

Usually, revenues exceed expenses resulting in income or a profit. When expenses exceed revenues, the difference is a loss.

Exercise 1-4   **Income and Losses.** A portion of North End Company's income statement for the year shows:

North End Company
Income for the year ended December 31, 20x0

Sales Revenue		$500,000
Expenses		
Cost of Goods Sold	$450,000	
Rent Expense	50,000	
Salaries	100,000	600,000
Income or loss		?

Which of the following reflects North End Company's income or loss?

a. $100,000 income
b. $500,000 income
c. $100,000 loss

> *Remember that losses result from expenses in excess of revenue (bad news).*

Solution   C. When expenses exceed revenues, income is negative. This is a loss.

Balance sheets

Balance sheets report the firm's situation at a particular point in time. While income statements show performance over a period of time, balance sheets give us a picture of the situation at a particular point in time. Balance sheet disclosures include assets, liabilities, and owners' equity.

Assets

Assets are items of value to the business. Examples include cash, inventories, investments, equipment, and buildings. Most of us are familiar with cash, investments, equipment, and buildings. Inventories are items purchased or manufactured for resale.

Specific balance sheet disclosures are referred to as accounts. For example, Cash, Investments, and Equipment on the balance sheet are accounts.

Liabilities

Liabilities are amounts owed. These are the creditor's claims against the business. One example is loans payable. The account titles of many liabilities include the word payable.

Exercise 1-5

Tip: Is the item valuable to the business (an asset) or does it reflect an obligation (a liability)?

Assets or Liabilities. Three of the following items are assets and three are liabilities. Indicate A (asset) or L (liability), as appropriate, for each item.

(A) L   Machinery
A (L)   Loan payable to a supplier
(A) L   Computer
A (L)   Loan payable to the bank
(A) L   Truck
A (L)   Loan payable to truck dealer

Solution

Machinery, computers, and trucks are assets. The other items are liabilities. Remember that assets are items of value. Machinery, computers, and trucks certainly fall into this category. Liabilities are amounts that the business owes.

Exercise 1-6

Assets and Liabilities. Anderson Company reports the following asset and liability accounts:

Anderson Company assets and liabilities
For the year ended December 31, 20x0

Cash	$ 60,000
Bank Loan Payable	70,000
Inventory	130,000
Buildings	100,000
Equipment	200,000

Which of the following is the amount of Anderson Company's total assets?

a. $490,000
b. $500,000
c. $530,000

Solution

C. All items except the bank loan payable are assets, items of value to the business. These four items total $490,000. The loan payable is a liability.

Owners' equity

Owners' equity is the third major component of the balance sheet. This is the owners' interest in the business. Owners' equity represents the owners' claims against the business assets. The two components of owners' equity are contributed capital and retained earnings.

Contributed capital

Contributed capital is the portion of owners' equity that owners contribute to the business. Owners of corporations hold shares of stock and are referred to as shareholders. One category of contributed capital is capital stock.

Example

Capital Stock. Everest Corporation began with a $20,000,000 investment from the owners who later contributed an additional $55,000,000. The Capital Stock account balance is now $75,000,000.

Everest Corporation
Changes in capital stock

Beginning Capital Stock	$20,000,000
Additional Investment	55,000,000
Ending Capital Stock	$75,000,000

Retained earnings

Retained earnings represent the second main component of owners' equity. Retained earnings increase as corporations earn income. Dividends are distributions of cash to shareholders. Declaring dividends reduces retained earnings.

Exercise 1-7

Retained Earnings. During the year, Valley Corporation's income is $300,000 and its dividends declared are $200,000. You can use the following table to find the increase in retained earnings.

Valley Corporation
Change in retained earnings

Add: Income	300,000
Less: Dividends Declared	200,000
Increase in Retained Earnings	100,000

Tip: Think of retained earnings as the earnings <u>retained</u> in the business (not declared as dividends).

Which of the following shows the increase in retained earnings?

a. $75,000
b. $100,000
c. $200,000

Solution

B. The increase in retained earnings is $100,000. This is the current period's income less the dividends declared.

Retained Earnings account balances are cumulative. For profitable companies, the balances typically increase every year.

Example

Retained Earnings. Prince Company begins the year with $900,000 of retained earnings and earns $500,000 during the year. Prince then declares dividends meaning that the company promises to distribute a certain amount of cash to owners. In this case, $300,000 is distributed. At the end of the year, retained earnings are $1,100,000 as follows:

Prince Company
Change in retained earnings

Beginning Retained Earnings	$ 900,000
Add: Income	500,000
Less: Dividends Declared	300,000
Ending Retained Earnings	$1,100,000

Note that dividends do not reduce income. Income measures financial performance, which is not influenced by dividend payments.

Exercise 1-8   **Retained Earnings**. Forest Corporation earns $90,000 in its first year, $120,000 in its second year, and $110,000 during the third year. Dividends declared are $60,000 each year.

Forest Corporation
Change in retained earnings

Beginning Retained Earnings $ 0

Add: Cumulative Income   320,000

Less: Dividends Declared   180,000

Ending Retained Earnings   140,000

Which of the following represents retained earnings at the end of the third year?

a. $30,000
b. $320,000
c. $140,000

Solution   C. Cumulative income increases retained earnings. Declaring dividends reduces retained earnings.

Forest Corporation
Change in retained earnings

Beginning Retained Earnings	$ 0
Add: Cumulative Income	320,000
Less: Dividends Declared	180,000
Ending Retained Earnings	$140,000

We know that ending retained earnings consists of beginning retained earnings plus income less dividends declared. Analysts can use this relationship to determine dividends or income given the other elements of retained earnings.

Exercise 1-9   **Retained Earnings**. Farmingdale Company begins the year with retained earnings of $50,000. During the year, the company earns $30,000. Ending retained earnings are $70,000. Use the following table to find the amount of dividends declared.

Farmingdale Company
Change in retained earnings

Beginning Retained Earnings	$50,000
Add: Cumulative Income	*30,000*
Less: Dividends Declared	*10,000*
Ending Retained Earnings	$70,000

Select the amount of dividends declared:

a. $5,000
b. $10,000
c. $30,000

Solution

B.   Retained earnings begin at $50,000. Income then adds $30,000, bringing the total to $80,000. Since the ending account balance is only $70,000, we know that dividends declared are $10,000.

Farmingdale Company
Change in retained earnings

Beginning Retained Earnings	$50,000
Add: Cumulative Income	30,000
Less: Dividends Declared	10,000
Ending Retained Earnings	$70,000

Exercise 1-10

Retained Earnings. Scoop Garden Company begins the year with retained earnings of $300,000. During the year, the company reports income. It then declares dividends of $25,000. Ending retained earnings are $325,000.

Scoop Garden Company
Change in retained earnings

Beginning Retained Earnings	$300,000
Add: Cumulative Income	*50,000*
Less: Dividends Declared	*25000*
Ending Retained Earnings	*325,000*

Scoop's income for the year is

a. $25,000.
b. $50,000.
c. $250,000.

Solution

B. Retained earnings increased from $300,000 to $325,000. The $25,000 in dividends declared, however, *reduces* retained earnings. Therefore, we know that income had to be $50,000.

Scoop Garden Company
Change in retained earnings

Beginning Retained Earnings	$300,000
Add: Income	50,000
Less: Dividends Declared	25,000
Ending Retained Earnings	$325,000

Review the previous examples until you're comfortable with these retained earnings exercises.

Exercise 1-11

Income, Dividends, and Retained Earnings. This exercise tests your ability to develop an income statement. Revenues, expenses, and dividends declared for Bread and Burger Inc., a restaurant chain, are as follows:

Bread and Burger Inc.
Income for the year ended December 31, 20x1

Sales Revenue	$1,500,000
Cost of Goods Sold	500,000
Rent Expense	300,000
Salaries	200,000
Dividends Declared	100,000

Income and the increase in retained earnings for 20x1 are

Remember that dividends declared never show on the income statement.

a. $500,000 and $400,000.
b. $400,000 and $400,000.
c. $400,000 and $0.

Solution

A. Income is $500,000. This is the revenue less the three expenses as shown on the following income statement:

Bread and Burger Inc.
Income for the year ended December 31, 20x1

Sales Revenue		$1,500,000
Cost of Goods Sold	$500,000	
Rent Expense	300,000	
Salaries	200,000	1,000,000
Income		$ 500,000

Retained earnings increase by $400,000 ($500,000 income less $100,000 dividends declared). Dividends declared reduce retained earnings but do not reduce income.

Please return to the beginning discussion of retained earnings and rework the previous exercises if you had trouble with this exercise.

Exercise 1-12

Owners' Equity. Owners of Southworth Corporation invested $200,000 to begin the business and an additional $600,000 in later years. Southworth Corporation earned $500,000 over the years and declared dividends of $100,000.

Which of the following are the correct balances in the Capital Stock and Retained Earnings accounts?

Tip: Remember that capital stock is the amount invested in the business and that retained earnings is cumulative earnings less dividends.

a. $200,000 and $400,000
b. $800,000 and $400,000
c. $1,200,000 and $0

Solution

B. Capital stock is the total amount invested in the business — $200,000 initially and $600,000 in later years for a total of $800,000. Southworth's retained earnings are $400,000, the cumulative earnings less dividends declared.

Southworth Corporation
Change in capital stock

Beginning Capital Stock	$200,000
Increases in Capital Stock	600,000
Ending Capital Stock	$800,000

Southworth Corporation
Change in retained earnings

Cumulative Income	$500,000
Less: Cumulative Dividends Declared	100,000
Ending Retained Earnings	$400,000

Go back to the contributed capital and retained earnings examples if you need help with this exercise.

A sample balance sheet

Earlier we looked at the income statement for Millennium Music Corporation, the record shop. Now we consider the corresponding balance sheet:

Millennium Music Corporation
Balance sheet at December 31, 20x0

Assets		Liabilities and Equity	
Cash	$ 75,000	Loan Payable	$ 20,000
Inventory	20,000	Capital Stock	120,000
Land	105,000	Retained Earnings	60,000
	$200,000		$200,000

Balance sheets and income statements always show the name of the business. This tells us that Millennium Music Corporation rather than some other entity holds the listed assets and is responsible for the liabilities. Similarly, income statements include only the income of the particular entity designated in the title of the statement. If owners have other sources of income or other assets, the other items are shown on separate financial statements for these businesses.

Tip: Remember to note the exact business name and date on financial statements.

In addition, balance sheets are always dated. This particular balance sheet shows account balances at the end of 20x0.

Exercise 1-13

Assets. Referring to Millennium's balance sheet, which of the following totals relates to items of value to the business?

a. $75,000
b. $95,000
c. $200,000

Solution

C. Cash, inventory, and land are all assets. These are the items of value to the business. The Loan Payable is a liability and Capital Stock is an owners' equity account.

Exercise 1-14

Owners' Equity. Select the correct amount of Millennium's owners' equity from the following choices:

> *Tip: If the account title says "payable," it isn't owners' equity.*

a. $120,000
b. $180,000
c. $200,000

Solution

B. The owners' equity accounts are Capital Stock ($120,000) and Retained Earnings ($60,000). These accounts reflect the owners' interest in the business. The loan payable is a liability and is not part of owners' equity.

Go back to the descriptions of capital stock and retained earnings if you missed this one.

The balance sheet equation

Assets, liabilities, and owners' equity are closely related. Reference to Millennium Music's balance sheet shows the following relationship:

Assets = Liabilities + Owners' Equity

The balance sheet equation relates assets and the claims against those assets. All balance sheets use this simple equation. Balance sheets serve at least two purposes. One is to show the various asset, liability, and owner's equity accounts. Another is to compare the claims against the company's assets.

Millennium Music's balance sheet shows two types of claims against the various assets. One is the bank loan, a liability. The other is owners' equity, the owners' interest. According to the balance sheet, assets are $200,000. Therefore, claims must also be $200,000. If the company discontinues business, the liabilities must be paid first. Claims by the owners always take a lower priority. Thus, if all assets are sold for only $150,000, lenders will receive $20,000 and the owners will receive the remaining $130,000.

An understanding of the balance sheet equation can be very useful in analysis. This is illustrated in the following example:

Example

The Balance Sheet. Assume that our copy of Millennium Music's annual report is damaged. We know the assets and liabilities but can't read the owners' equity portion. If we know the assets ($200,000) and liabilities ($20,000), we can use the balance sheet equation to calculate owners' equity.

$$\text{Assets} = \text{Liabilities} + \text{Owners' Equity}$$

$$\$200,000 = \$20,000 + \text{Owners' Equity}$$

Subtracting $20,000 from both sides leaves the following:

$$\$200,000 - \$20,000 = \text{Owners' Equity} = \$180,000$$

Exercise 1-15

Balance Sheet Relationships. Assume that Street Corporation has liabilities of $80,000 and owners' equity equal to $50,000. Using the Assets = Liabilities + Owners' Equity relationship, what is the amount of the assets?

$A = L + OE = 80000 + 50,000 = 130,000$

Solution

The assets are $130,000. We know that liabilities and owners' equity total $130,000. Since Assets = Liabilities + Owners' Equity, assets must also equal $130,000.

Exercise 1-16

Balance Sheet Relationships. Portions of Washington Corporation's balance sheet were damaged by a coffee spill. Luckily, we were able to read all items except those designated with question marks.

Washington Corporation
Balance sheet at December 31, 20x1

Assets		Liabilities and Equity	
Cash	$ 50,000	Bank Loan Payable	$?
Inventory	400,000	Capital Stock	100,000
Land	20,000	Retained Earnings	200,000
	$470,000		$?
			470,000

Our challenge is to determine the Bank Loan Payable balance. A two-step approach is recommended. First use the balance sheet equation to find the total amount of liabilities and owners' equity. Then calculate the liabilities. Which of the following is the correct choice for Washington's Loan Payable?

a. $50,000
b. $170,000
c. $200,000

Solution

B. Since Assets = Liabilities + Owners' Equity, we know that the total liabilities and owners' equity must be the same as the assets, $470,000. Then, since owners' equity totals $300,000 (capital stock plus retained earnings), the $170,000 remaining balance must reflect the bank loan. The complete balance sheet is as follows:

Washington Corporation
Balance sheet at December 31, 20x1

Assets		Liabilities and Equity	
Cash	$ 50,000	Bank Loan Payable	$170,000
Inventory	400,000	Capital Stock	100,000
Land	20,000	Retained Earnings	200,000
	$470,000		$470,000

Exercise 1-17

Assets and Liabilities. All of Boston Company's balance sheet accounts except Retained Earnings are shown here:

Boston Company
Balance sheet accounts at December 31, 20x0

Cash	$ 40,000
Bank Loan Payable	30,000
Inventory	50,000
Equipment	200,000
Capital Stock	100,000
Note Payable for Equipment	60,000
Buildings	400,000
Retained Earnings	?

Our interest is in knowing the Retained Earnings account balance. For this exercise we should first classify the accounts as assets, liabilities, or owners' equity. Then we can use the balance sheet equation to calculate the missing amounts.

Boston Company's Retained Earnings account balance is

a. $230,000.
b. $500,000.
c. $600,000.

Solution

B. Retained earnings are $500,000. Assets (cash, inventory, equipment, and buildings) total $690,000. This means that liabilities and owners' equity must also be $690,000. Since the two payables total $90,000, owners' equity must be $600,000. Of this, $100,000 is capital stock. Thus, retained earnings are $500,000. Boston Company's complete balance sheet shows the following:

Boston Company
Balance sheet at December 31, 20x0

Assets		Liabilities and Equity	
Cash	$ 40,000	Bank Loan Payable	$ 30,000
Inventory	50,000	Note Payable	60,000
Equipment	200,000	Capital Stock	100,000
Buildings	400,000	Retained Earnings	500,000
	$690,000		$690,000

Exercise 1-18

Balance Sheet Relationships. Judy Jones started a small business at the end of 20x0 by investing her own cash and borrowing $15,000 from friends. At this point, the business has $20,000 cash and no other assets.

a. How much of her own money did Judy invest?   5,000 (20,000 - 15,000)

b. Prepare the balance sheet at the end of 20x0.

c. The balance sheet shows two sources of claims on the business assets. Which group of claims has first payment priority?

Jones Corporation
Balance sheet at December 31, 20x0

Assets		Liabilities and Equity	
Cash	20,000	Loans Payable	15,000
		Capital Stock	5,000
		Total	20,000

Solution

a. Judy invested $5,000 of her own money. We know this because assets are $20,000, and liabilities are $15,000. Since Assets = Liabilities + Owners' Equity, owners' equity must be $5,000. Owners' equity, in this case, is composed solely of Judy's contributed capital because the business has not had an opportunity to generate retained earnings.

b. The balance sheet shows these relationships as follows:

Jones Corporation
Balance sheet at December 31, 20x1

Assets		Liabilities and Equity	
Cash	$20,000	Loans Payable	$15,000
		Capital Stock	5,000
			$20,000

c. The two groups of claims are liabilities and owners' equity. Liabilities have the first payment priority. If the business dissolves, the owners may receive funds only after all liabilities are paid.

Money measure-ment

You may have noticed that all the events identified for Millennium Music Corporation are expressed in terms of dollars. This is a necessary condition for reporting items in the financial statements.

Unfortunately, some important events or conditions are difficult to express in dollars. Examples include the health of the company president and the satisfaction of customers. Consequently, these items cannot be recorded as transactions in the accounting system. This money measurement principle is one limitation of accounting. It means that the accounts do not reflect some items of interest to the company and to users of financial statements. Thus, analysts must go beyond accounting disclosures to truly understand a business. Accounting information, however, is an excellent starting point for business analysis.

Exercise 1-19

Identification of Transactions. Knight Corporation operates a chain of videotape rental stores. Recently, the company noticed that its inventory of tapes is not as extensive as that of its competitors. Knight's accountant does not include this potentially important information in the financial statements for the following reasons:

a. Inventory does not show in the accounts.
b. The accounts are adjusted only when cash is received or paid.
c. The money measurement principle.

Solution   C. The money measurement principle prevents the accountant from recording information that is not easily expressed in dollar amounts. Knight and other companies show their inventory at cost. We know that choice a is incorrect because inventory is an important balance sheet item. Choice b is also incorrect because we also know that many important accounting adjustments do not involve cash receipts or payments.

**Summary
of key
points**

income

Income is a measure of financial performance.
Income measures performance over a specified period.
The income statement includes revenues and expenses.
Revenues result from providing services.
Expenses result from the use of services.
If expenses exceed income, the business has a loss.
Dividends are distributions to shareholders.
Income is *not* reduced for dividends.

**The
balance
sheet**

Assets are items of value to the business.
Liabilities are the creditor's claims, the amounts owed.
Owners' equity reflects the owners' claims, the owners' interest.
Contributed capital (capital stock) is the amount that owners have contributed to the business.
Retained earnings increase with income and decrease with dividends declared.

**Money
measure-
ment
principle**

The money measurement principle means that accounting statements show only those events and situations that can be expressed in terms of dollars. Other items, such as the quality of products, are not reflected directly in the accounts.

Chapter 2

Recording what happened (Transactions)

People in business refer to events recorded in the accounting system as <u>transactions</u>. The first step in the accounting process is to analyze transactions.

Learning objectives

The objectives of this chapter include the following:

- To analyze and classify transactions.
- To reinforce your understanding of the asset, liability, and owners' equity relationship.
- To learn how transactions relate to the income statement and balance sheet.
- To learn how to use T-accounts, a useful tool in financial analysis.

Analyzing transactions

Earlier we looked briefly at an income statement and balance sheet for Millennium Music Corporation, a store that sells records, tapes, and CDs. The following transactions occurred during Millennium's first year in business:

1.	Cash Contributed to the Business by Shareholders	$120,000
2.	Cash Paid for Inventory of Records, Tapes, and CDs	110,000
3.	Merchandise Sold for Cash	240,000
4.	Cost of Goods Sold to Customers	90,000
5.	Borrowed from the Bank	20,000
6.	Cash Expenses Incurred	80,000
7.	Land Purchased for Cash	105,000
8.	Dividends Declared and Paid to Shareholders	10,000

As you work this chapter, you will learn to analyze transactions and prepare income statements and balance sheets. One central concept is that transactions lead to changes in either assets, liabilities, or owners' equity. In addition, you will discover that all transactions concern two or more accounts. You already know that

Assets = Liabilities + Owners' Equity

Another simple but important principle follows:

All transactions have at least two components.

You'll see how these concepts work as you study Millennium Music Corporation's transactions.

1. **Cash Contributed to the Business by Shareholders**. The first transaction is the owners' contribution of cash to the business. As a rule, businesses begin with cash contributions from the owners. When the business receives $120,000 from the owners, assets increase and owners' equity also increases. The asset is Cash and the owners' equity item is Capital Stock. This transaction satisfies the balance sheet equation, Assets = Liabilities + Owners' Equity. At this point, the balance sheet shows the asset and the owners' claim against the asset. In tabular form this is:

Additions to both assets and owners' equity maintain the balance sheet relationship.

Description	Assets	Liabilities	Equity
Cash Contributed by Shareholders	$120,000		$120,000

2. **Cash Paid for Inventory of Records, Tapes, and CDs**. This transaction involves the $110,000 purchase of inventory for cash. Two assets are involved. One is cash. Cash payments reduce assets. The other side of the transaction is the increase in inventory. This part of the transaction increases assets. Total assets, however, do not change nor do liabilities and owners' equity. When the company acquires inventory for cash, it replaces one asset with another asset.

Increasing one asset and decreasing another also maintains the balance sheet equality.

Description	Assets	Liabilities	Equity
Cash Paid for Inventory	$110,000		
	-$110,000		

Note that even though the business spends a great deal of cash, it does not record an expense. Expenses reflect the use of services. In this case, the expense comes later when the goods are sold.

3. **Merchandise Sold for Cash**. The third transaction concerns $240,000 of cash sales. The relevant accounts are Cash and Sales Revenue. Sales revenue increases income and income, in turn, increases retained earnings. Thus, Sales Revenue is an owners' equity account. We already know that receiving cash increases assets.

Description	Assets	Liabilities	Equity
Merchandise Sold for Cash	$240,000		$240,000

Exercise 2-1

The Balance Sheet Equation. For each of the three transactions, we were careful to be sure that Assets = Liabilities + Owners' Equity. Consequently, this relationship must hold true for the total of the three transactions. The transactions considered to date are grouped in the following table. Sum the assets, liabilities, and owners' equity to be sure that the balance sheet balances.

	Description	Assets	Liabilities	Equity
1	Cash Contributed by Shareholders	$120,000		$120,000
2	Cash Paid for Inventory	110,000		
		-110,000		
3	Merchandise Sold for Cash	240,000		240,000
	Totals	360,000		360,000

Solution

At this point, the business has $360,000 in total assets and $360,000 in total owners' equity. The accounts balance.

	Description	Assets	Liabilities	Equity
1	Cash Contributed by Shareholders	$120,000		$120,000
2	Cash Paid for Inventory	110,000		
		-110,000		
3	Merchandise Sold for Cash	240,000		240,000
	Totals	$360,000		$360,000

Remember that expenses reduce owners' equity.

4. **Cost of Goods Sold.** Transaction 3 recognized sales revenue. Now we consider an offsetting factor — the $90,000 expense pertaining to inventory usage — the cost of the goods that were sold. The cost of goods sold reduces income and owners' equity. Expenses reflect the use of services. Since much of the inventory was sold, the transaction recognizes the reduction in inventory and in owners' equity.

Description	Assets	Liabilities	Equity
Cost of Goods Sold	-$90,000		-$90,000

Exercise 2-2

Borrowed from the Bank. You should have a pretty good idea of how to record transactions based on your work to this point. The next transaction is the $20,000 bank loan. This increases cash as well as another balance sheet category, an amount owed. Based on your understanding of asset and liability relationships, complete the following table.

Description	Assets	Liabilities	Equity
Borrowed from the Bank	20,000	20,000	0

Solution

The bank loan increases cash and establishes a liability. Your entries should appear as follows:

Description	Assets	Liabilities	Equity
Borrowed from the Bank	$20,000	$20,000	0

The next exercise concerns expenses, the use of services. Think of expenses as the opposite of revenues. Previously, we considered the cost of goods sold expense. That transaction reduced assets and owners' equity. The following exercise concerns other expenses for cash, a transaction that also reduces assets and owners' equity.

Exercise 2-3

Cash Expenses Incurred. Complete the following table to reflect $80,000 in expenses and payments.

Description	Assets	Liabilities	Equity
Cash Expenses Incurred	-80,000		- 80,000

Solution

Cash payments reduce assets. Expenses reduce income, a component of owners' equity.

Description	Assets	Liabilities	Equity
Cash Expenses Incurred	-$80,000		-$80,000

Exercise 2-4

Land Purchased for Cash. This transaction is similar to the purchase of inventory (transaction 2) in that one asset increases and another asset decreases. Complete the following table to show the purchase of land for $105,000.

> *Note that buying land is not an expense.*

Description	Assets	Liabilities	Equity
Land Purchased for Cash	105,000		
	- 105,000		

Solution

The transaction showing the payment of cash in exchange for land follows:

Description	Assets	Liabilities	Equity
Land Purchased for Cash	*$105,000*		
	-$105,000		

Exercise 2-5

Declaring dividends reduces owners' equity.

Dividends Declared and Paid to Shareholders. The last event is the declaration and payment of cash dividends amounting to $10,000. As indicated previously, dividends are distributions of cash to the owners. Earlier you learned that retained earnings increase with income. Retained earnings decrease when dividends are declared. Thus, one side of this transaction is concerned with the reduction of owners' equity to reflect dividends declared. You also know that cash, an asset, decreases when the dividends are paid. The transaction to reflect dividends declared and paid is as follows:

Description	Assets	Liabilities	Equity
Dividends Declared and Paid	- 10,000		- 10,000

Solution

The declaration and payment of dividends reduce both assets and owners' equity as follows:

Description	Assets	Liabilities	Equity
Dividends Declared and Paid	*-$10,000*		*-$10,000*

The following table summarizes progress to this point.

	Description	Assets	Liabilities	Equity
1	Cash Contributed by Shareholders	$120,000		$120,000
2	Cash Paid for Inventory	110,000		
		-110,000		
3	Merchandise Sold for Cash	240,000		240,000
4	Cost of Goods Sold	-90,000		-90,000
5	Borrowed from the Bank	20,000	$20,000	
6	Cash Expenses Incurred	-80,000		-80,000
7	Land Purchased for Cash	105,000		
		-105,000		
8	Dividends Declared and Paid	-10,000		-10,000
	Totals	$200,000	$20,000	$180,000

If assets equal liabilities and owners' equity for each transaction, total assets will equal total liabilities and owners' equity.

The company's assets total $200,000. As expected, total liabilities and owners' equity also equal $200,000. Since you checked to be sure that each transaction balances, the totals must also balance.

At this point, we could prepare an income statement and balance sheet. However, we would need reference to the original events because our summary shows only whether the transactions increase or decrease assets, liabilities, or owners' equity. It does not show whether an adjustment to equity, for example, changes income or contributed capital.

We will now record the same eight events using a system that is more powerful than our simple row and column approach. Although transaction analysis is common to both approaches, the system to be presented provides for recording transactions in specific accounts.

T-accounts

T-accounts help us to organize and analyze transactions.

One deficiency of the simple row and column approach is that it doesn't show which specific accounts are associated with asset, liability, and owners' equity items. We now learn how the system of T-accounts helps accountants summarize transactions and prepare financial statements. This system shows the information necessary to prepare the income statement and balance sheet. Once the data are recorded, it won't be necessary to refer to the original events.

We'll continue to work with the eight events considered previously. These are summarized as follows:

1	Cash Contributed by Shareholders	$120,000
2	Cash Paid for Inventory	110,000
3	Merchandise Sold for Cash	240,000
4	Cost of Goods Sold	90,000
5	Borrowed from the Bank	20,000
6	Cash Expenses Incurred	80,000
7	Land Purchased for Cash	105,000
8	Dividends Declared and Paid	10,000

1. **Cash Contributed by Shareholders**. We already know that this transaction increases cash and increases capital stock. In addition, we know that cash is an asset and that capital stock is an owners' equity item. This transaction is recorded in two T-accounts. T-accounts are named after their shape which is similar to the letter T. One account is for Cash and the other is for Capital Stock.

Cash		Capital Stock	
120,000			120,000

Notice that the entry for Cash shows on the left side of the T-account. Capital Stock shows on the right. This is consistent with three simple but important rules:

Increases in assets go on the left.

Increases in liabilities or owners' equity are opposite.

Lefts = Rights

This last relationship means that entries on the left equal entries on the right.

You shouldn't need to memorize these simple rules. Practice with the exercises will make their application automatic.

2. **Cash Paid for Inventory**. Previously, you determined that inventory increased while cash decreased for this transaction. Since increases in assets show on the left, we record the increase in inventory on the left-hand side. Then, since lefts equal rights, we need a right-side entry. Our right-side entry is to Cash as follows:

Cash		Capital Stock	
120,000			120,000
	110,000		

Inventory	
110,000	

Why does the adjustment to cash go on the right side? We know that increases in assets go on the left. Decreases are the opposite. Thus, this transaction illustrates a corollary to the basic rule for recording transactions.

The basic rule is

increases in assets go on the left.

The corollary is

decreases are the opposite.

If increases show on one side of an account, decreases show on the other.

One helpful feature of recording items in accounts is that we can easily obtain the account balances. Examination of the Cash account, for example, shows that the remaining amount is $10,000 ($120,000 offset by $110,000).

3. **Merchandise Sold for Cash**. Here the company records $240,000 as sales revenue and the receipt of cash. Since cash is an asset, the entry to Cash is on the left side. Earning revenue increases income (and retained earnings) and is shown on the opposite side, the right side.

Cash		Capital Stock	
120,000			120,000
	110,000		
240,000			

Inventory		Sales Revenue	
110,000			240,000

Accountants work with right-side and left-side balances all the time and have assigned names to these entries:

Debits are left-side entries.

Credits are right-side entries.

Thus, an entry to increase cash is called a <u>debit</u>. An entry to reduce assets is called a <u>credit</u>. Since lefts = rights,

debits = credits

Note that debits and credits don't mean good or bad. The only meaning is left or right.

Exercise 2-6

> *Remember that expenses and other reductions of owners' equity are left-side entries.*

Cost of Goods Sold. The cost of the goods sold to customers is $90,000. We know that the cost of goods sold is an expense, an income and owners' equity account. The other part of the transaction recognizes the reduction in inventory that was sold. Using your knowledge of left-side and right-side entries, show how the following T-accounts reflect the cost of goods sold and adjustment to inventory.

Solution

We debit the Cost of Goods Sold account because the expense reduces income (and owners' equity). Increases in owners' equity are credits; they go on the right. Decreases are the opposite.

Inventory is credited because this transaction reduces assets. Increases in assets go on the left. This decrease is on the opposite side. The completed accounts are as follows:

Cash			Capital Stock	
120,000				120,000
	110,000			
240,000			Sales Revenue	
				240,000
Inventory				
110,000			Cost of Goods Sold	
	90,000		*90,000*	
20,000				

Millennium Music Corporation has drawn a horizontal line in the Inventory account and entered the $20,000 Inventory account balance. This means that remaining inventory is $20,000.

Exercise 2-7

Borrowed from the Bank. We learned previously, that the $20,000 bank loan increases both assets and liabilities. Show the entries to record this transaction.

Cash		Loan Payable	Capital Stock
120,000			120,000
	110,000	*20, 000*	
240,000			Sales Revenue
20,000			240,000

Inventory		Cost of Goods Sold
110,000		90,000
———	90,000	
20,000		

Solution

The increase in cash, of course, is a left-side entry, a debit. Since increases in liabilities and owners' equity items go on the right, we credit the Loan Payable account.

Cash		Loan Payable	Capital Stock
120,000			120,000
	110,000	*20,000*	
240,000			Sales Revenue
20,000			240,000

Inventory		Cost of Goods Sold
110,000		90,000
———	90,000	
20,000		

Exercise 2-8   **Cash Expenses Incurred.** Event number six reflects cash expenses of $80,000.

Remember that expenses reduce owners' equity and consequently show on the debit side. Record the expense and cash payment.

Cash		Loan Payable		Capital Stock	
120,000			20,000		120,000
	110,000				
240,000				**Sales Revenue**	
20,000					240,000
	80,000				
				Cost of Goods Sold	
				90,000	
Inventory					
110,000				**Cash Expenses**	
	90,000			*80,000*	
20,000					

Solution   The following shows the reduction of owners' equity and cash for $80,000 in expenses. We debit Other Expenses to reflect the reduction in owners' equity. Cash is credited because the transaction also reduces assets.

Cash		Loan Payable		Capital Stock	
120,000			20,000		120,000
	110,000				
240,000				**Sales Revenue**	
20,000					240,000
	80,000				
				Cost of Goods Sold	
				90,000	
Inventory					
110,000				**Cash Expenses**	
	90,000			*80,000*	
20,000					

Exercise 2-9   **Land Purchased for Cash.** The company purchased land for $105,000.

Since we previously recorded the inventory purchase, it should be straightforward to record the similar exchange of land for cash.

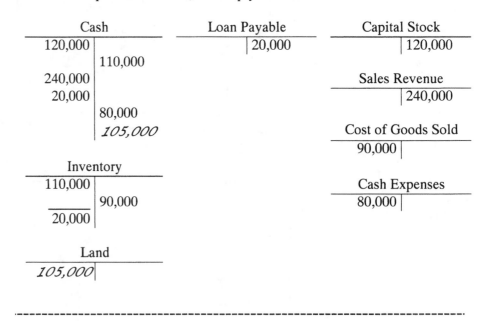

Cash		Loan Payable	Capital Stock
120,000	110,000	20,000	120,000
240,000			
20,000			
	80,000		
	105,000		

Solution   To record the purchase of land, we simply debit land and credit cash.

Cash		Loan Payable	Capital Stock
120,000	110,000	20,000	120,000

(T-accounts showing: Cash 120,000 / 110,000; 240,000; 20,000 / 80,000; / 105,000. Inventory 110,000 / 90,000; 20,000. Land 105,000. Loan Payable / 20,000. Capital Stock / 120,000. Sales Revenue / 240,000. Cost of Goods Sold 90,000. Cash Expenses 80,000.)

Exercise 2-10   **Dividends Declared and Paid**.   Finally, the company declares and pays $10,000 in cash dividends. This entry reduces both cash and owners' equity. The specific owners' equity entry is a debit to Dividends Declared. Your challenge is to make this entry and then to show the balance in the cash account.

Dividend Declared Dr
Cash Cr.

Cash		Loan Payable	Capital Stock
120,000			20,000		120,000
	110,000			
240,000			**Sales Revenue**
20,000				240,000
	80,000		
	105,000		**Cost of Goods Sold**
	10,000		90,000	
			Cash Expenses
Inventory			80,000	
110,000			
	90,000		**Dividends Declared**
20,000			*10,600*	
Land			
105,000			

Solution   The complete set of accounts follows. Cash is credited in this transaction because payment reduces the asset. Dividends Declared is debited because this action reduces owners' equity.

Millennium Music's cash balance is $75,000, the net amount of the various debit and credit entries to this account.

Cash		Loan Payable	Capital Stock
120,000			20,000		120,000
	110,000			
240,000			**Sales Revenue**
20,000				240,000
	80,000		
	105,000		**Cost of Goods Sold**
_____	*10,000*		90,000	
75,000			
			Cash Expenses
Inventory			80,000	
110,000			
_____	90,000		**Dividends Declared**
20,000			*10,000*	
Land			
105,000			

Classification

When we recorded transactions the first time, we entered only the effect on assets, liabilities, or owners' equity. The ending balances by account category are as follows:

Balance by account category

Assets	$200,000
Liabilities	$ 20,000
Owners' Equity	180,000
Total	$200,000

With T-accounts, however, we can easily develop a more informative list of accounts. Summarizing account balances for the preceding list of T-accounts provides the following additional detail:

Account balances

Assets		
Cash	$ 75,000	
Inventory	20,000	
Land	105,000	$200,000
Liabilities		$ 20,000
Owners' Equity		
Capital Stock	$120,000	
Sales Revenue	240,000	
Cost of Goods Sold	-90,000	
Other expenses	-80,000	
Dividends Declared	-10,000	180,000
Total		$200,000

Journal entries

We know how to record transactions with T-accounts. A second approach uses journal entries. The debits and credits are the same with either method. Journal entries show all sides of the transaction in one place. In contrast, when a large number of T-accounts are used, it's difficult to find all parts of the transaction. Thus, it is often helpful to record journal entries.

We just learned how to record eight transactions in T-account format. The first six transactions are as follows:

1.	Cash Contributed by Shareholders	$120,000
2.	Cash Paid for Inventory	110,000
3.	Merchandise Sold for Cash	240,000
4.	Cost of Goods Sold	90,000
5.	Borrowed from the Bank	20,000
6.	Cash Expenses Incurred	80,000

1. **Cash Contributed by Shareholders**. We know that the debit is $120,000 to Cash and the credit is to Capital Stock. The journal entry format is as follows:

Cash	*120,000*	
Capital Stock		*120,000*

As indicated previously, this is just another way to record the transaction examined in the T-account framework. Debits continue to go on the left and credits continue to go on the right. The corresponding numbers show in left and right columns. One advantage is that it is fairly easy to tell if debits don't equal credits. Another is that it's easy to see both sides of the transaction. Note that the debit comes first and that the credit is indented. Journal entries are always done this way. Debits are first; credits follow.

2. **Cash Paid for Inventory**. When the company acquires inventory for cash, it debits inventory and credits cash for $110,000. In journal entry form the transaction appears as follows:

Inventory	*110,000*	
Cash		*110,000*

Exercise 2-11

Merchandise Sold for Cash. Try recording cash and sales revenue of $240,000.

Cash   240,000

Sales Revenue   240,000

Solution

Your journal entry should appear as follows:

Cash	*240,000*	
Sales Revenue		*240,000*

Note that the debit showing the increase in cash is recorded first. Following this, and indented, the accountant shows the credit to increase owners' equity.

Exercise 2-12

Miscellaneous Journal Entries. Now record the following three events in journal format.

Cost of Goods Sold	$90,000
Borrowed from the Bank	20,000
Cash Expenses Incurred	80,000

Cost of Goods Sold   90,000
    Inventory   90,000

Cash   20,000
    Loans payable   20,000

Cash expenses   80,000
    Cash   80,000

Solution

Your journal entries should show the following:

Cost of Goods Sold	90,000
Inventory	90,000
Cash	20,000
Loan Payable	20,000
Cash Expenses	80,000
Cash	80,000

Please refer to the corresponding T-accounts examined earlier for questions about any of these entries. The account titles, debits, and credits are identical for T-accounts and journal entries. Only the form of the entry differs.

Summary of key points

Transactions are events of interest in the accounting system.

The accounting process begins with identifying and recording transactions.

All transactions have at least two components.

With respect to entries in the accounts
Increases in assets go on the left.
Increases in other items are the opposite.
Decreases in assets are also opposite.
Lefts = Rights

Accountants call the left-side and right-side entries debits and credits.
Debits are left-side entries.
Credits are right side-entries.
Debits = Credits

Since individual transactions always balance, the total of all transactions must also balance.

Journal entries are an alternative way to show the parts of a transaction. The principle of debits and credits is the same with T-accounts and journal entries.

Exercise 2-13   **Evaluating Events and Recording Transactions**. CopyRight, Inc., a new copy service, just opened this year.   During the year, the following events occurred:

1.	Cash Contributed by Shareholders	$ 20,000
2.	Cash Paid for Paper and Supplies Inventory	35,000
3.	Merchandise Sold for Cash	220,000
4.	Cost of Goods Sold	30,000
5.	Borrowed from Parents and Friends	25,000
6.	Cash Rent and Salary Expenses Incurred	140,000
7.	Dividends Declared and Paid	40,000

Your mission is to refer to the preceding example when necessary and record these seven transactions (1) in journal entries and (2) in T-accounts. Then develop the list of account balances.

Journal Entries. Enter the appropriate accounts in the spaces indicated:

1. Cash Contributed by Shareholders

    Cash   20,000

        Capital Stock   20,000

2. Cash Paid for Paper and Supplies Inventory

    Inventory   35,000

        Cash   35,000

3. Merchandise Sold for Cash

    Cash   220,000

        Sales Revenue   220,000

4. Cost of Goods Sold

    Cost of goods sold   30,000

        Inventory   30,000

5. Borrowed from Parents and Friends

| Cash | 25,000 | |
| Loans payable | | 25,000 |

6. Cash Rent and Salary Expenses Incurred

| Rent & Salary exp. | 140,000 | |
| Cash | | 140,000 |

7. Dividends Declared and Paid

| Dividends Declared | 40,000 | |
| Cash | | 40,000 |

T-accounts. Now record the same transactions in the following T-accounts:

Cash		Loan Payable	Capital Stock
20,000	35,000	25,000	20,000
220,000			
25,000	140,000		Sales Revenue
	40,000		220,000
50,000			Cost of Goods Sold
			30,000

Inventory		Dividends Declared
35,000	30,000	40,000
5000		Rent and Salary Expense
		140,000

The List of Account Balances. Finally, show the account balances summarized from your T-accounts:

Account balances

Assets

Cash	50,000	
Inventory	5,000	55,000
Liability		25,000

Owners' Equity

Capital Stock	20,000	
Sales Revenue	220,000	
Cost of Goods Sold	-30,000	
Rent and Salary	-140,000	
Dividends Declared	-40,000	30,000
Total		55,000

Solutions

1. **Cash Contributed by Shareholders**. Capital stock is an owners' equity account. The debit reflects the increase in the asset and the credit is to the increase in owners' equity as follows:

Cash	20,000	
Capital Stock		20,000

2. **Cash Paid for Paper and Supplies Inventory**. In this case, one asset increases and another asset decreases:

Inventory	35,000	
Cash		35,000

3. **Merchandise Sold for Cash**. The debit is to Cash and the credit is to Sales Revenue reflecting the increase in owners' equity.

Cash	220,000	
Sales Revenue		220,000

4. **Cost of Goods Sold**. The cost of goods sold expense reduces equity. Inventory is also reduced because it is sold.

Cost of Goods Sold	30,000	
Inventory		30,000

5. **Borrowed from Parents and Friends**. With this transaction, both assets and liabilities increase as follows:

Cash	25,000	
Loan Payable		25,000

6. **Cash Rent and Salary Expenses Incurred**. The expenses reduce owners' equity while the cash payment reduces assets.

Rent and Salary Expense	140,000	
Cash		140,000

7. **Dividends Declared and Paid**. Declaring dividends reduces owners' equity. The payment reduces assets.

Dividends Declared	40,000	
Cash		40,000

T-accounts. Your T-accounts should appear as follows:

Cash		Loan Payable		Capital Stock	
20,000			25,000		20,000
	35,000				
220,000				**Sales Revenue**	
25,000					220,000
	140,000				
	40,000			**Cost of Goods Sold**	
50,000				30,000	

Inventory		Dividends Declared	
35,000		40,000	
	30,000		
5,000		**Rent and Salary Expense**	
		140,000	

The Account Balances. Based on the preceding T-accounts, the account balances are as follows:

Account balances

Assets		
Cash	$ 50,000	
Inventory	5,000	$55,000
Liability		$25,000
Owners' Equity		
Capital Stock	20,000	
Sales Revenue	220,000	
Cost of Goods Sold	-30,000	
Rent and Salary	-140,000	
Dividends Declared	-40,000	30,000
Total		$55,000

Chapter 3

Preparing for next year
(Closing the books)

One function of accounting is to measure performance over a specified time period, which may be a month, a quarter, or a year. Analysts are particularly interested in quarterly and annual income.

After recording all transactions for the year, accountants close the books. Closing the books provides for the following:

- To determine annual income.
- To set revenue and expense account balances to zero at the end of the accounting period in preparation for next year.
- To calculate retained earnings.
- To prepare the balance sheet.

The procedure is extremely important, but it is quite simple. Mechanically, closing the books consists of transferring balances from one account to another. This chapter illustrates the closing process.

Learning objectives

The objectives of this chapter include the following:

- To identify permanent and temporary accounts and to know which accounts should be closed.
- To close revenue and expense accounts.
- To work with the Income Summary and Dividends Declared accounts.
- To use the closing process to develop retained earnings.
- To understand the cost, conservatism, and going concern principles.

Permanent accounts

Accounts are classified as either permanent or temporary. Permanent accounts maintain their balances beyond the end of the accounting year. Nearly all asset and liability accounts are permanent. Capital Stock and Retained Earnings accounts are also in this category.

Example

Permanent Accounts. Missile Systems Corporation's Cash and Equipment account balances are $50,000 and $220,000, respectively, at the end of Year 1. These accounts are permanent because the account balances continue into the following year. Missile System's books continue to show the same Cash and Equipment account balances on January 1 as on the previous December 31.

Temporary accounts

Revenue accounts, expense accounts, and the Dividends Declared account are referred to as temporary accounts. At the end of the business year, accountants always set the balances of temporary accounts to zero. In this way, income measurement begins with a fresh start each year.

Example   **Temporary Accounts**. Delicious Bakery Corporation's Sales Revenue and Cost of Goods Sold account balances are $500,000 and $350,000, respectively. These are temporary accounts and are closed at the end of the business year. Closing the accounts ensures that each year's income includes revenues and expenses only for that year. Delicious begins each January 1 with a clean slate; all revenue and expense accounts are zero.

Exercise 3-1   **Permanent and Temporary Accounts**. Borden Motor Corporation ends the year with account balances that include the following:

Tip: Permanent account balances continue to the next year.

Account	Amount
Cash	$ 21,000
Sales Revenue	900,000
Equipment	160,000
Salary Expense	88,000
Accounts Payable	75,000

Identify the permanent and temporary accounts.

Solution   Cash, Equipment, and Accounts Payable are permanent accounts; they are not closed at the end of the year. The Sales Revenue and Salary Expense accounts must be closed to determine income and to ensure that the beginning balances of these accounts for the following year are zero.

The closing process   In the previous chapter, we recorded transactions for Millennium Music Corporation, the record shop. Now we will close the books and prepare the corporation's income statement and balance sheet. Key steps in the closing process are as follows:

1. Identify permanent and temporary accounts.
2. Close all revenue and expense accounts to Income Summary, a new account.
3. Close Income Summary to Retained Earnings.
4. Close Dividends Declared to Retained Earnings.

Example   **Closing Temporary Accounts**. From the previous chapter, after recording all transactions, the T-account balances for Millennium Music Corporation are as follows:

Cash	Loan Payable	Sales Revenue
75,000	| 20,000	| 240,000

Inventory	Capital Stock	Cost of Goods Sold
20,000	| 120,000	90,000 |

Land	Dividends Declared	Other Expenses
105,000	10,000 |	80,000 |

The first step in closing is to identify permanent and temporary accounts. All of Millennium Music's asset and liability accounts are permanent. Permanent accounts also include Capital Stock and Retained Earnings. We ignore these accounts when closing. This means that closing does not affect Millennium's assets or liabilities. Closing does not change the total owners' equity balance. Only the composition of specific owners' equity accounts changes with closing entries.

This leaves the following four temporary accounts to be closed:

Sales Revenue
Cost of Goods Sold
Other Expenses
Dividends Declared

Note that the four temporary accounts net to $60,000 as follows:

Account	Amount
Sales Revenue	$240,000
Cost of Goods Sold	-90,000
Other Expenses	-80,000
Dividends Declared	-10,000
Net	$ 60,000

When we finish, we'll see that retained earnings increase by $60,000.

Example   **Close All Revenue and Expense Accounts**. Continuing the previous example, we close all revenue and expense accounts. First we transfer the revenue and expense account balances to a new account called <u>Income Summary</u>. We close Sales Revenue by debiting Sales Revenue and crediting Income Summary as follows:

Cash	Loan Payable	Sales Revenue
75,000		20,000			240,000

240,000 in Sales Revenue debit column; balance *0*

Inventory	Capital Stock	Cost of Goods Sold
20,000		120,000	90,000

Land	Dividends Declared	Other Expenses
105,000		10,000		80,000

Income Summary

| 240,000 |

Now the $240,000 balance in Sales Revenue shows in the Income Summary account. Sales Revenue is closed. Next year Sales Revenue will accumulate starting from zero.

Closing the expense accounts uses the same rationale. Since expense accounts have left-side balances, these balances move to the left side of Income Summary. To close the Cost of Goods Sold account, we debit Income Summary and credit Cost of Goods Sold as follows:

Cash	Loan Payable	Sales Revenue
75,000		20,000	240,000	240,000
		0

Inventory	Capital Stock	Cost of Goods Sold
20,000		120,000	90,000	
			90,000
		0	

Land	Dividends Declared	Other Expenses
105,000		10,000		80,000

Income Summary

| | 240,000 |
| *90,000* | |

Both Sales Revenue and the Cost of Goods Sold accounts now have zero balances. The previous balances, $240,000 and $90,000, were transferred to Income Summary.

Exercise 3-2

Tip: Reference to the previous section on Cost of Goods Sold should help with this procedure.

Closing Other Expenses. The procedure for closing Other Expenses is the same as for closing Cost of Goods Sold. Practice the closing process by closing Other Expenses; then calculate the new balance for Income Summary.

Cash		Loan Payable		Sales Revenue	
75,000			20,000		240,000
				240,000	
					0

Inventory		Capital Stock		Cost of Goods Sold	
20,000			120,000	90,000	
					90,000
				0	

Land		Dividends Declared		Other Expenses	
105,000		10,000		80,000	
					80000
				0	

Income Summary	
	240,000
90,000	
80,000	
	70,000

Millenium Music Corp
Income Summary for the year
ended Dec. 31st, 20x0

Sales Revenue		240,000
Expenses		
COGS	90,000	
Other exps.	80,000	170,000
Income		70,000

Solution Your solution should show a debit to Income Summary and a credit to Other Expenses. The account balance for Other Expenses is now zero. Income Summary has a $70,000 balance:

Cash		Loan Payable		Sales Revenue	
75,000			20,000		240,000
				240,000	
					0

Inventory		Capital Stock		Cost of Goods Sold	
20,000			120,000	90,000	
					90,000
				0	

Land		Dividends Declared		Other Expenses	
105,000		10,000		80,000	
					80,000
				0	

Income Summary	
	240,000
90,000	
80,000	
	70,000

The balance in Income Summary is the company's income. For our purposes, we can think of the Income Summary account as our income statement. It shows the same numbers as the chart examined earlier.

Millennium Music Corporation
Income for the year ended December 31, 20x0

Sales Revenue		$240,000
Expenses		
Cost of Goods Sold	$90,000	
Other Expenses	80,000	170,000
Income		$ 70,000

Example

Close Income Summary to Retained Earnings. Now we close Income Summary to Retained Earnings, an owners' equity account. We debit Income Summary and credit Retained Earnings as follows:

Cash	Loan Payable	Sales Revenue
75,000	20,000	240,000
		240,000
		0

Inventory	Capital Stock	Cost of Goods Sold
20,000	120,000	90,000
		90,000
		0

Land	Dividends Declared	Other Expenses
105,000	10,000	80,000
		80,000
		0

Retained Earnings	Income Summary
70,000	240,000
	90,000
	80,000
	70,000
	70,000
	0

At this point, Dividends Declared is the only remaining temporary account. We know that retained earnings increase with income and decrease with dividends declared. Thus, the final step is to close Dividends Declared to Retained Earnings.

Exercise 3-3

Closing Dividends Declared. Since Dividends Declared has a debit balance, the closing entry requires a credit to this account and a debit to Retained Earnings. Show this entry in the following accounts:

Cash		Loan Payable		Sales Revenue	
75,000			20,000		240,000
				240,000	
					0

Tip: Always close Dividends Declared directly to Retained Earnings.

Inventory		Capital Stock		Cost of Goods Sold	
20,000			120,000	90,000	
					90,000
				0	

Land		Dividends Declared		Other Expenses	
105,000		10,000		80,000	
			10,000		80,000
		0		0	

Retained Earnings		Income Summary	
	70,000		240,000
10,000		90,000	
		80,000	
	60,000		70,000
		70,000	
			0

Solution

After debiting Retained Earnings and crediting Dividends Declared, the accounts appear as follows:

Cash		Loan Payable		Sales Revenue	
75,000			20,000		240,000
				240,000	
					0

Inventory		Capital Stock		Cost of Goods Sold	
20,000			120,000	90,000	
					90,000
				0	

Land		Dividends Declared		Other Expenses	
105,000		10,000		80,000	
			10,000		80,000
		0		0	

Retained Earnings		Income Summary	
	70,000		240,000
10,000		90,000	
	60,000	80,000	
			70,000
		70,000	
			0

Note: All temporary accounts are closed. We have a balance sheet!

All remaining accounts with non-zero balances are permanent accounts. These permanent accounts compose the balance sheet.

At this point, all temporary accounts are closed. We have developed both an income statement and the ending balance for Retained Earnings. Recall that we began by calculating the net amount of the four temporary accounts, $60,000. We now see that $60,000 is the addition to Retained Earnings. (Since the firm did not have beginning retained earnings, $60,000 is also the ending Retained Earnings account balance.) Thus, the balances in the temporary accounts do not disappear, but are merely transferred to Retained Earnings, a balance sheet account.

Why use an income summary account?

You might wonder why we bother setting up Income Summary accounts that are closed later. We could ignore this step and close directly to Retained Earnings. Our procedure ensures that only income accounts are included in calculating income, the measure of financial performance. The Income Summary account also serves as our income statement. One account that is never included in income summary is Dividends Declared. Dividends are distributions of cash to owners and financial performance is measured before providing for dividends. Following the steps outlined here helps to ensure against erroneously reducing income by the amount of dividends.

The balance sheet

We know that one objective of closing is to provide a balance sheet. You can test your understanding of the balance sheet with the following exercise.

Exercise 3-4

How the Numbers Get Onto the Balance Sheet. Our T-accounts correspond exactly with Millennium Music's balance sheet:

Balance sheet for Millennium Music Corporation
At December 31, 20x0

Assets		Liabilities and Equity	
Cash	$ 75,000	Loan Payable	$ 20,000
Inventory	20,000	Capital Stock	120,000
Land	105,000	Retained Earnings	60,000
	$200,000		$200,000

The balance sheet provides answers to a number of important questions. With respect to Millennium Music's balance sheet

Tip: We record assets at cost.

a. What is the original cost of Millennium's assets? *200,000*

b. How much of the inventory remains at year-end? *20,000*

c. How much does Millennium Music owe at the end of the year? *20,000*

Tip: Capital stock is the amount invested; owners' equity includes retained earnings.

d. How much have the business owners invested since the business began? *120,000*

e. What is the owners' claim on the business assets? *180,000 (120,000 + 60,000)*

Solutions

a. Millennium Music's assets originally cost $200,000, which is the amount shown for total assets.

b. The cost of ending inventory is shown as $20,000 which is the inventory that remains after subtracting the cost of goods sold.

c. Liabilities are $20,000 — the loan payable.

d. Capital stock is $120,000, the amount invested by the owners.

e. Owners' equity is the owners' claim. The amount is $180,000, which consists of capital stock and retained earnings.

| Key measure-ment concepts | Now that we understand the basics of the accounting system, we should consider key concepts in income measurement. Important principles that govern the measurement of income statement and balance sheet items include the cost principle, conservatism, and the going concern assumption. |

Cost principle

Most assets including inventories, buildings, and equipment are recorded on the books at their historical cost. Accountants do not usually attempt to show these items at market values. One reason for this is that accounting information may be more reliable to users if it is based on easily verifiable information that is not subject to disagreement. Although people may agree on the costs of assets, they are less likely to agree on market values. This means that persons who are interested in the current values of assets must look to sources other than financial statements for this information. We have already made extensive use of the cost principle in previous examples and exercises.

Exercise 3-5

Tip. Financial statements show most assets at cost.

Cost Principle. Undeveloped land originally costing $400,000 is now worth $3,000,000. The land will show on the balance sheet at

a. $400,000.
b. $3,000,000.
c. some other amount.

Solution

A. Land generally shows at its original cost.

Principle of conser-vatism

Accountants are trained to take a conservative approach when recording assets and liabilities. Therefore, when in doubt, accountants record assets at lower amounts and record liabilities at higher amounts. For example, if the ability to collect receivables becomes doubtful, accountants generally reduce the amounts at which these assets show on the books. Of course, they still attempt to collect the amounts due. Similarly, when accountants expect future obligations such as payments of health benefits to retired employees, they record liabilities for these amounts. This is done even though future changes in health plans may reduce benefit payments to lower amounts.

Example

Conservatism Principle. Ivory Systems Corporation produces its I5001 model computers at an average cost of $1,200 and shows its inventory of unsold computers on the books at this amount. Due to price reductions for computer chips and hard drives, Ivory finds that it could manufacture the same computer

Hint: Assets are sometimes shown at less than cost.

today for only $1,000. Following the principle of conservatism, Ivory Systems should reduce the carrying value of inventory to the $1,000 current cost.

Going concern assumption

The <u>going concern assumption</u> is a third important concept. People in business generally assume that businesses will continue to operate as going concerns. Therefore, equipment and other assets show on the books at historical cost or adjusted historical cost.

Example

Smith Manufacturing Corporation just invested in special-purpose equipment costing $2,000,000. The equipment works well, but since it is special purpose, it has no resale value. Smith shows the equipment at $2,000,000 on its balance sheet because the company expects to benefit through the use of the equipment and does not expect to dispose of it.

Exercise 3-6

Measurement Concepts. Amalgamated Appliance Company just learned that Pay-Mart Corporation, a major customer, has run short of cash and has declared bankruptcy. Pay-Mart's prices were so low that the company couldn't earn a profit. Amalgamated is concerned that it will not collect a $1,000,000 receivable from Pay-Mart. This will not threaten Amalgamated's ability to remain in business, but it may reduce the company's cash flow. In accord with <u>generally accepted accounting principles</u>, the company reduces the receivable to a lower amount. This is an application of

Tip: The issue at hand is the adjustment of receivables.

a. the concept that revenue is recorded when services are provided.
b. the principle of conservatism.
c. the going concern assumption.

Solution

B. The principle of conservatism suggests writing the receivables down to a lower amount. This principle holds that when in doubt, assets should be shown at lower amounts and liabilities should be shown at higher amounts.

While revenue is recorded in the accounts when services are provided, this is not the main issue here. The issue presented in this case relates to the adjustment of assets. Choice c is not the most appropriate choice since Amalgamated's ability to continue as a going concern has not been questioned. Therefore, b seems to be the best choice.

**Summary
of key
points**

The closing process consists of four steps:

1. Identify permanent and temporary accounts.
2. Close all revenue and expense accounts to Income Summary, a new account.
3. Close Income Summary to Retained Earnings.
4. Close Dividends Declared to Retained Earnings.

Closing accomplishes several purposes. It sets all temporary account balances to zero in preparation for the next accounting period, it calculates income and retained earnings, and it develops a balance sheet. The Income Summary account serves as an income statement. Use of a separate Income Summary account helps to ensure that dividends are not closed to income.

We also learned about the cost principle, the principle of conservatism, and the going concern assumption. The cost principle holds that assets are generally recorded at their historic cost; usually the purchase price. The principle of conservatism encourages accountants not to overstate the recorded amounts of assets and equity. In applying the going concern assumption, accountants generally assume that businesses will continue to operate as going concerns and consequently do not record assets at expected liquidation amounts.

Exercise 3-7   **Closing Revenue and Expense Accounts.** After recording all transactions for 20x5, WinSome Company's books show various permanent and temporary accounts. Beginning with the following account balances, close all revenue and expense accounts to Income Summary.

Cash	Loan Payable	Sales Revenue
25,000		10,000			300,000

300,000   *0*

Inventory	Capital Stock	Cost of Goods Sold
10,000		40,000	170,000	

170,000

Investments	Dividends Declared	Other Expenses
50,000		4,000		100,000	

100,000   *0*

	Retained Earnings	Income Summary
		9,000		

170,000 300,000
100,000
30,000

Solution

The three income statement accounts are Sales Revenue, Cost of Goods Sold, and Other Expenses. Since Sales Revenue has a right-side balance, the $300,000 amount moves to the right side of Income Summary. Cost of Goods Sold and Other Expenses both have debit balances that move to the debit side of income summary. Income summary is the net amount, $30,000. This is basically the company's income statement.

Cash	Loan Payable	Sales Revenue
25,000		10,000			300,000
				300,000	
					0

Inventory	Capital Stock	Cost of Goods Sold
10,000		40,000		170,000	
					170,000
				0	

Investments	Dividends Declared	Other Expenses
50,000		4,000		100,000	
					100,000
				0	

	Retained Earnings	Income Summary
		9,000			*300,000*
			170,000	
			100,000	
				30,000

Exercise 3-8 **Closing Income Summary and Dividends Declared.** In the previous exercise, we closed WinSome Company's revenue and expense accounts. Now our challenges are to close Income Summary and Dividends Declared to Retained earnings and to prepare a balance sheet.

Close the Income Summary and Dividends Declared accounts to Retained Earnings and complete the company's balance sheet.

Cash		Loan Payable		Sales Revenue	
25,000			10,000		300,000
				300,000	
					0

Inventory		Capital Stock		Cost of Goods Sold	
10,000			40,000	170,000	
					170,000
				0	

Investments		Dividends Declared		Other Expenses	
50,000		4,000		100,000	
			4,000		100,000
		0		0	

Retained Earnings		Income Summary	
	9,000		300,000
4000	*30,000*	170,000	
	35,000	100,000	
			30,000
		30,000	

Balance sheet for Winsome Company
At December 31, 20x5

Assets		Liabilities and Equity	
Cash	*25,000*	Loan Payable	*10,000*
Inventory	*10,000*	Capital Stock	*40,000*
Investments	*50,000*	Retained Earnings	*35,000*
Total	*85,000*	Total	*85,000*

Solution The final two steps are to close Income Summary and Dividends Declared to Retained Earnings. First transfer the Income Summary's credit balance to Retained Earnings. Then transfer the $4,000 Dividends Declared balance to the debit side of Retained Earnings. Your T-accounts should appear as follows:

Cash	Loan Payable	Sales Revenue
25,000		10,000			300,000
			300,000	
				0

Inventory	Capital Stock	Cost of Goods Sold
10,000			40,000	170,000	
				170,000
			0	

Investments	Dividends Declared	Other Expenses
50,000		4,000		100,000	
			4,000		100,000
		0		0	

Retained Earnings	Income Summary
	9,000		300,000
		170,000	
		100,000	
			30,000
	30,000	*30,000*	
4,000			*0*
	35,000	

This results in the following balance sheet.

Balance sheet for Winsome Company
At December 31, 20x5

Assets		Liabilities and Equity	
Cash	$25,000	Loan Payable	$10,000
Inventory	10,000	Capital Stock	40,000
Investments	50,000	Retained Earnings	35,000
	$85,000		$85,000

Hint: Remember that retained earnings are cumulative.

Note that Winsome Company began the year with a $9,000 balance in retained earnings. When we add the current year's income and subtract dividends declared, retained earnings increase by $26,000. Thus, the ending retained earnings balance is $35,000.

Exercise 3-9	**Comprehensive Transaction Analysis and Closing the Books.** Firststar Shipping Company had the following transactions during 20x2:

1.	Revenues	$750,000
2.	Salary Expense	400,000
3.	Interest Revenue from Investments	40,000
4.	Other Expenses	90,000
5.	Dividends Declared	85,000
6.	Dividends Paid	80,000

Tip: Dividends declared increase dividends payable. Paying dividends reduces the payable.

Transactions 1 through 4 are very similar to the ones that you previously recorded. Please review the earlier material if you have questions. Transactions 5 and 6 concern dividends. When the company declares dividends, it announces a promise to pay, a liability. Some of these dividends may be paid in the following year. Thus, the declaration of dividends is reported as follows:

Dividends Declared	85,000
Dividends Payable	85,000

The current year's payment then removes the liability as follows:

Dividends Payable	80,000
Cash	80,000

Beginning balances are shown in the following T-accounts. Record the transactions, close the books, and calculate retained earnings after all closing entries.

Balance Sheet for Firstar Shippin Co.
On Dec. 31st 20x2

Assets
Cash	260,000
Investments	460,000
	720,000

Liabilities & OE
Div. payable	5,000
Capital Stk.	70000
Retained earngs	645000
	720,000

> *This exercise has beginning balances. Note that beginning assets equal beginning liabilities plus equity, a necessary condition.*

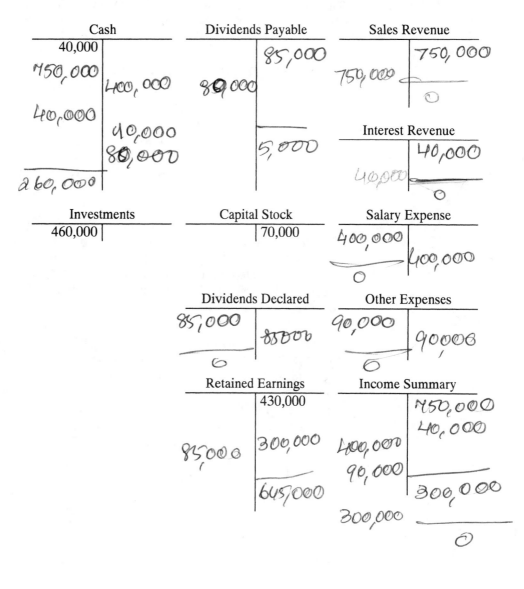

Cash	
40,000	
750,000	400,000
40,000	
	40,000
	80,000
260,000	

Dividends Payable	
	85,000
80,000	
	5,000

Sales Revenue	
	750,000
750,000	
	0

Interest Revenue	
	40,000
40,000	
	0

Investments	
460,000	

Capital Stock	
	70,000

Salary Expense	
400,000	400,000
0	

Dividends Declared	
85,000	85,000
0	

Other Expenses	
90,000	90,000
0	

Retained Earnings	
	430,000
85,000	300,000
	645,000

Income Summary	
	750,000
	40,000
400,000	
90,000	
	300,000
300,000	
	0

Solution   The balance sheet follows. Note that revenues, expenses, and the Dividends Declared account do not appear on balance sheets. These temporary accounts are always closed to Retained Earnings.

Balance sheet for Firststar Shipping Company
At December 31, 20x2

Assets		Liabilities and Equity	
Cash	$260,000	Dividends Payable	$ 5,000
Investments	460,000	Capital Stock	70,000
		Retained Earnings	645,000
	$720,000		$720,000

Remember that temporary accounts do not appear on balance sheets.

Firststar's balance sheet shows cash and other items of value totaling $720,000. This means that liabilities and owners' equity must also equal $720,000. This is so because Assets = Liabilities + Equity is a necessary condition for any balance sheet. Of the three liability and equity items, dividends payable is the single liability.

If your ending balances correspond to these and your income is $300,000, you understand the closing procedure and should move to the next chapter. If you prefer to confirm the details, the solution follows in stages beginning with the day-to-day transactions. After recording the six transactions, the T-accounts show the following:

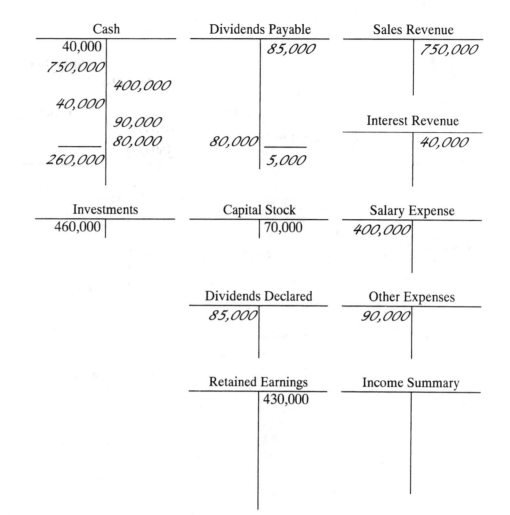

Cash		Dividends Payable		Sales Revenue	
40,000			85,000		750,000
750,000					
	400,000				
40,000					
	90,000			**Interest Revenue**	
	80,000	80,000			40,000
260,000			5,000		

Tip: Dividends Payable, a liability, always shows a right-side balance.

Investments		Capital Stock		Salary Expense	
460,000			70,000	400,000	

Dividends Declared		Other Expenses	
85,000		90,000	

Retained Earnings		Income Summary	
	430,000		

Following the recommended procedure, Firststar first closes the revenue and expense accounts to Income Summary. Income is $300,000, as shown in the subtotal for Income Summary. Then Income Summary and Dividends Declared are closed to Retained Earnings. The closing entries to Income Summary are as follows:

Cash		Dividends Payable		Sales Revenue	
40,000			85,000		750,000
750,000				*750,000*	
	400,000				*0*
40,000					
	90,000			Interest Revenue	
	80,000	80,000			40,000
260,000			5,000	*40,000*	
					0

Investments		Capital Stock		Salary Expense	
460,000			70,000	400,000	
					400,000
				0	

		Dividends Declared		Other Expenses	
		85,000		90,000	
					90,000
				0	

		Retained Earnings		Income Summary	
			430,000		*750,000*
					40,000
				400,000	
				90,000	
					300,000

The remaining entries to develop retained earnings entail closing the Income Summary and Dividends Declared accounts as follows:

Cash		Dividends Payable		Sales Revenue	
40,000			85,000		750,000
750,000				750,000	
	400,000				0
40,000					
	90,000			**Interest Revenue**	
	80,000	80,000			40,000
260,000			5,000	40,000	
					0

Investments		Capital Stock		Salary Expense	
460,000			70,000	400,000	
					400,000
				0	

		Dividends Declared		Other Expenses	
		85,000		90,000	
			85,000		90,000
		0		0	

		Retained Earnings		Income Summary	
			430,000		750,000
					40,000
				400,000	
				90,000	
					300,000
			300,000	*300,000*	
		85,000			0
			645,000		

Firststar has closed all temporary accounts. The remaining accounts are permanent, meaning that they show on the balance sheet. The balance sheet corresponds exactly to the preceding accounts.

Note: Review the earlier material if you have questions or if your accounts do not correspond with the ones shown.

Chapter 4

Income isn't always cash
(Accrual basis accounting)

In nearly all of the transactions examined to this point, we recorded revenues and expenses when cash was received or paid. In practice, however, services are sometimes provided or received at one point in time and cash is collected or paid earlier or later. Accrual basis accounting refers to differences in the timing of income statement items and cash receipts or payments. In other words, revenue and expense recognition does not always correspond to the timing of cash receipts and payments. This chapter illustrates common accrual basis accounting transactions. These transactions relate to sales and purchases on account, interest income and expense, and other expenses.

Learning objectives

The objectives of this chapter include the following:

- To learn the principles and importance of accrual basis accounting.
- To understand receivable and payable accounts.
- To work with compound entries.

Accounts receivable

Businesses usually ship goods to commercial customers before receiving payment. For example, customers might be given 30 days to pay for goods. One reason for this is that the buyer and seller don't actually meet when goods are shipped by truck or rail.

Example

Goods Sold on Account. Maxwell Manufacturing Corporation ships goods valued at $90,000 to Franchise Industries, Inc., with payment due in 25 days. Maxwell's journal entry at the time of shipment follows:

Accounts Receivable	90,000	
Sales Revenue		90,000

Accounts receivable are assets. Receivables are valuable assets because in most cases, they quickly become cash. When payment is received, the seller makes this entry:

Cash	90,000	
Accounts Receivable		90,000

Note that we record revenue when services are provided (goods are shipped).

In T-account form, the initial entry to record sales revenue and the receivable is as follows:

Accounts Receivable	Cash	Sales Revenue
90,000		90,000

When the cash is received, this entry is made:

Note that when goods are sold on account, revenue is not recorded when cash is received.

Accounts Receivable		Cash		Sales Revenue
90,000	90,000	90,000		90,000
0				

Since cash receipts tend to follow sales, the balance sheets of businesses that sell on account show accounts receivable at all points in time. New receivables continuously replace old receivables that are collected. An example follows.

Example

Continuing Sales on Account. Church Corporation sells goods on account during the year for $80,000. Collections this year are $50,000. Next year, sales on account are $75,000 and collections are $70,000. For the first year, Church's T-accounts show the following:

Accounts Receivable		Cash		Sales Revenue
80,000	50,000	50,000		80,000
30,000				

The entries for Year 2 follow:

Note: Businesses that sell on account always show receivables on the balance sheet.

Accounts Receivable		Cash		Sales Revenue
30,000				
75,000	70,000	70,000		75,000
35,000				

Note the relationship between the Accounts Receivable balance, cash received, and sales revenue. In the first year, Accounts Receivable increases by $30,000. This is the difference between revenue and cash received. Similarly, in the second year, the account balance increases by $5,000 (from $30,000 to $35,000) because Year 2 sales revenue also exceeds the cash collected that year.

Exercise 4-1

Accounts Receivable. Increases in accounts receivable represent the current year's sales not yet collected. Which is true for decreases in accounts receivable?

a. Decreases in receivables usually mean that cash collections exceed the current period's sales.

Tip: Changes in receivables mean that cash collections differ from revenue.

b. Decreases in receivables usually mean that cash collections are less than the current period's sales.

c. Changes in receivables are hard to interpret.

Solution

A. When accounts receivable decrease, the business has collected more cash than the current year's sales. Choice b is incorrect because it's the opposite.

To illustrate this, assume that Sweet Corporation, a manufacturer of iced tea products, begins the year with $100,000 in receivables. During the year, Sweet sells beverages on account for $700,000 and collects $740,000 from customers. Since collections exceed sales by $40,000, receivables decrease by $40,000 to $60,000, as shown in the following T-accounts:

Accounts Receivable		Cash		Sales Revenue	
100,000					
700000	*740,000*	*740,000*			*700,000*
60,000					

Exercise 4-2

Sales on Account. This exercise concerns relationships between the Accounts Receivable, Cash, and Sales Revenue accounts.

During Year 1, French Company sells goods on account for $80,000. Collections are $60,000. Sales on account in Year 2 are $90,000 and collections are $85,000. Show the T-account entries and calculate the ending balance in Accounts Receivable.

Year 1

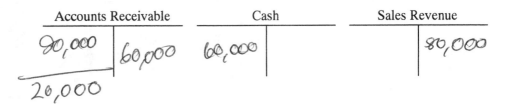

Accounts Receivable		Cash		Sales Revenue	
90,000	*60,000*	*60,000*			*80,000*
20,000					

Year 2

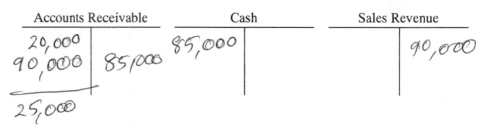

Accounts Receivable		Cash		Sales Revenue	
20,000		85,000			90,000
90,000	85,000				
25,000					

Solution Each year, accounts receivable increase with sales and decrease with cash collections. The completed accounts for Year 1 are as follows:

Year 1

Accounts Receivable		Cash		Sales Revenue	
80,000		60,000			80,000
	60,000				
20,000					

The first entry shows $80,000 sales revenue and the increase in accounts receivable. Then accounts receivable are reduced as the company collects cash.

Year 2

Accounts Receivable		Cash		Sales Revenue	
20,000		85,000			90,000
90,000					
	85,000				
25,000					

Purchases on account When one party sells goods on account, the other party pays on account. Sellers record <u>Accounts Receivable</u> and buyers record <u>Accounts Payable</u>. Earlier we examined the sale of goods on account by Maxwell Manufacturing Corporation. Now, we consider Franchise Industries, Inc., the buyer.

Example **Purchases on Account**. Maxwell Manufacturing Corporation ships goods valued at $90,000 to Franchise Industries, Inc., with payment due in 25 days. Franchise's journal entries to record the receipt of goods and the later payment follow:

Inventory	90,000	
Accounts Payable		90,000
Accounts Payable	90,000	
Cash		90,000

T-account form follows:

Cash	Inventory	Accounts Payable
	90,000	90,000
90,000		90,000
		0

Note that the buyer's entries are essentially a mirror image of the entries made by the seller. One party shows receivables and the other shows payables. Similarly, one receives cash and the other pays cash.

Exercise 4-3

Purchases on Account. This exercise illustrates relationships between the Cash, Inventory, and Accounts Payable accounts.

Topeka Company buys goods on account during Year 1 for $40,000. Payments this year are $35,000. During Year 2, purchases are $60,000 and payments are $55,000. The assignment is to record these transactions and calculate ending balances.

Note that the amount paid for inventory is rarely the same as the purchases on account.

Year 1

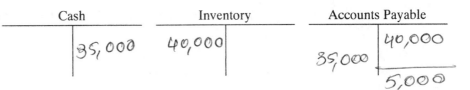

Cash	Inventory	Accounts Payable
35,000	40,000	40,000
		35,000
		5,000

Year 2

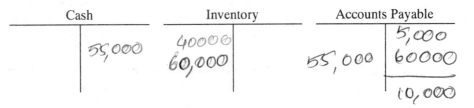

Cash	Inventory	Accounts Payable
55,000	40000	5,000
	60,000	55,000 / 60000
		10,000

Solution

Accounts payable increase with purchases and decrease as payments are made. T-accounts for each of the two years show that accounts payable increase to $5,000 at the end of the first year and by an additional $5,000 at the end of Year 2.

Year 1

Cash	Inventory	Accounts Payable
	40,000	40,000
35,000		35,000
		5,000

Year 2

Cash		Inventory		Accounts Payable	
		40,000			5,000
		60,000			60,000
	55,000			55,000	
					10,000

Topeka Company should also have sold much of its inventory. We ignore the inventory account for this problem since the purpose is to focus on purchases and accounts payable.

Other expenses

Other common expense accruals relate to wages, utility expenses, and interest. The treatment of these items is similar to the treatment of accounts payable.

Wages payable

Wages payable are amounts due to employees at the end of the accounting period. Typically, employees work for one or more weeks before they are paid. Consequently, an employee who starts work early in December may receive only one paycheck for the month with the second check due in early January. The employer will, however, record wage expense for the services used for the full month.

Example

Wages Payable. Randy Smith begins work at Walnut Corporation on December 1, 20x4. His $4,000 per month salary is payable every two weeks. Due to the time necessary to process paperwork, Walnut writes Randy's first paycheck amounting to $3,000 on December 26 representing three weeks of work. The next check is scheduled for early January 20x5.

The company used Randy's services for the full month and should record wage expense of $4,000. Since Walnut Corporation paid only $3,000 during 20x4, the remainder of the $4,000 expense is payable next year. This remaining amount shows on the balance sheet as Wages Payable, a liability.

Entries to record the expense, the liability, and the cash payment follow:

Wage Expense	4,000	
Wages Payable		4,000
Wages Payable	3,000	
Cash		3,000

This leaves an ending liability of $1,000 developed in T-account format as follows:

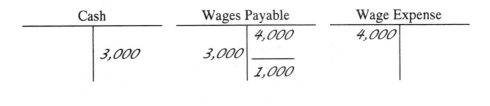

	Cash		Wages Payable			Wage Expense	
				4,000		4,000	
		3,000	3,000	———			
				1,000			

- -

Exercise 4-4

Tip: Wages payable increase with wage expense and decrease with payments to workers.

Wages Payable. Harrison Corporation begins and ends the year with the Wages Payable account balances shown in the following T-accounts. During the year, wage expense is $400,000. How much did the company pay its employees?

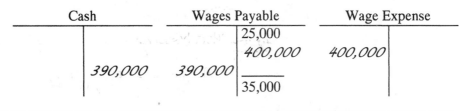

	Cash		Wages Payable			Wage Expense	
				25,000			
	390,000	390,000	390,000	400,000		400,000	
				35,000			

Solution

Payments to employees must have been $390,000. We know that companies initially record the $400,000 wages earned as both an expense and a liability. Companies then reduce this liability when they pay the workers. Paying employees is the only way to reduce the liability for wages payable.

We started with beginning wages payable of $25,000 and increased this when we recorded the $400,000 expense. Then the only way to end the year with a $35,000 liability is to pay the workers $390,000. If we substitute other amounts for the payments, the ending liability will not be $35,000. In other words, nothing else works!

	Cash		Wages Payable			Wage Expense	
				25,000			
				400,000	400,000		
	390,000	390,000	390,000	———			
				35,000			

- -

Compound entries

In the previous example, we recorded wage expense and the payment as two separate entries. Alternatively, we could use a compound entry. We know that all transactions must have at least two parts to maintain the balance sheet equality. Compound entries have more than two parts.

Example

The Compound Entry. Harrison Corporation's wage expense is $400,000 with $390,000 actually paid to workers during the year. We know that the following entries apply:

Wage Expense	400,000	
Wages Payable		400,000
Wages Payable	390,000	
Cash		390,000

A compound entry accomplishes the same purpose more concisely as follows:

Wage Expense	400,000	
Cash		390,000
Wages Payable		10,000

The convention, as with any journal entry, is to record the debit first. Credits are indented. If there is more than one debit or credit account, all debits come first followed by all credits. Compound entries involve less writing than single entries. Another advantage in this case is that the compound entry clearly shows the $10,000 increase in the Wages Payable account balance.

Exercise 4-5

Compound Entries. During the year, English Chocolate Company purchases inventory on account for $140,000 and pays $110,000 to suppliers. First complete the account titles; then show these transactions as one compound entry.

With two simple entries, first record purchases:

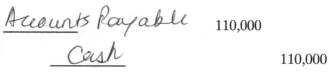

Inventory	140,000
Accounts Payable	140,000

Then record payments:

Accounts Payable	110,000
Cash	110,000

Revise, as a compound entry:

Inventory	140,000
Cash	110,000
Accounts Payable	30,000

Solution

With two simple entries:

Inventory	140,000	
Accounts Payable		140,000
Accounts Payable	110,000	
Cash		110,000

The company debits inventory to reflect the increase in assets. The $140,000 credit to Accounts Payable, a liability, reflects the promise to pay for the goods. The company then reduces the liability when it pays the supplier $110,000. Since accounts payable increase by $30,000 ($140,000 owed for purchases less $110,000 paid), the entries can be summarized in compound form as follows:

Inventory	140,000	
Cash		110,000
Accounts Payable		30,000

Note again that the debit always comes first and that both credits follow. Since the company bought and paid for inventory at different times, it would actually use the two-entry approach in this case.

Other expenses payable

Many expenses including those relating to electricity, long-distance telephone charges, and other expenses are routinely paid on account. Businesses (and individuals) typically delay payment until the bill is due.

Exercise 4-6

Expenses Payable. This is the first year of business for Sawtooth Company. During the year, Sawtooth received telephone bills amounting to $300,000. The last bill for $40,000 was received on December 22 and is payable in January. Consequently, only $260,000 of the $300,000 in expenses were paid during the year. Show a simple entry to record the phone bills received for the year and a second simple entry to record the payments. Then show the same transactions using a compound entry.

The bills received:

Phones/Utilities exp   300,000

  Expenses payable   300,000

The payments made:

Expenses payable 260,000

 Cash   260,000

Hint: Accounting for accounts payable and expenses payable is basically the same.

The compound entry made:

Phone/utility exp 300,000

 Cash   260,000

 Exp. payable 40,000

Solution

The following are the two simple entries to record the expense and make payments:

Phone or Utilities Expense	300,000	
Expenses Payable		300,000

Expenses Payable	260,000	
Cash		260,000

Expenses payable increased by $40,000 during the year. The expense increases the liability by $300,000; payments reduce it by $260,000. In compound form, the entries are as follows:

Phone or Utilities Expense	300,000	
Cash		260,000
Expenses Payable		40,000

If you are comfortable with the preceding exercise, you understand both expenses payable and compound entries.

Exercise 4-7

Expenses Payable. Congo Company has been in business for several years. At the beginning of the year, the Expenses Payable account for electricity was $70,000. During the year, the company received electric bills for $600,000 and paid $620,000. Show T-accounts to reflect the transactions relating to electricity use for the year. (Hint: Utilities send bills when they provide services. Thus, the bill from the utility reflects the use of electric services, an expense.)

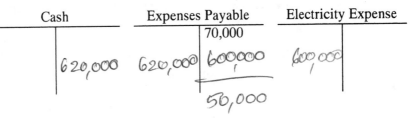

Solution

Since the company paid $20,000 more than the amount billed, the Expenses Payable account balance falls by this amount to $50,000. Congo received bills for $600,000 and presumably used services in the same amount. Thus, utility expense is $600,000. You could work this exercise using either two simple entries or one compound entry.

As two simple entries:

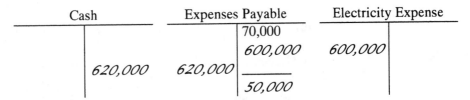

With one compound entry:

Cash		Expenses Payable		Electricity Expense	
			70,000		
620,000		20,000	_____	600,000	
			50,000		

Although it would have been easier to use journal entries for this problem, T-accounts help us visualize the relationships between the balance sheet and income statement. They also make it easy to calculate ending balances. Both journal entries and T-accounts help you to learn the accounting system and analyze changes in accounts.

Accruals for interest

Interest receivable and payable accruals are also common. Loans typically earn interest on a continuous basis. The interest may be paid only periodically, however.

Example

Interest Payable. SouthCentral Corporation borrows $200,000 on April 1 by issuing 10 percent bonds payable. The annual interest at 10 percent is $20,000. Following the usual custom, these bonds pay $10,000 interest twice per year. Since SouthCentral borrows on April 1, semi annual interest payments are due at the end of March and September.

On April 1, Year 1, SouthCentral makes the following entry to record the receipt of cash and loan payable:

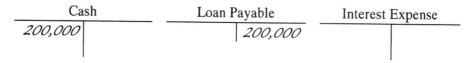

Cash	Loan Payable	Interest Expense
200,000	200,000	

It makes the first interest payment at the end of September:

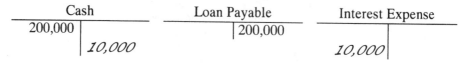

Cash	Loan Payable	Interest Expense
200,000	200,000	
10,000		10,000

At this point, three months remain to the end of the year.

In late December, SouthCentral accrues interest from September to the end of the year because the company used services (borrowed funds) until the end of the year. As a result, $5,000 — the interest for three months — shows as an additional expense for the year and a liability on December 31:

Cash	Loan Payable	Interest Expense
200,000	200,000	10,000
10,000		
	Interest Payable	
	5,000	5,000
		15,000

Note that this entry ensures that the expense is recognized when the services are used.

Thus, interest expense — the use of services from April 1 to December 31— is $15,000. Since the payment for Year 1 was only $10,000, $5,000 shows as interest payable, a liability. At the end of Year 1, Interest Expense is closed to Income Summary.

Now we consider Year 2. At the beginning of Year 2, the Interest Expense account balance is zero. The liability accounts, however, are all permanent. Account balances for the liabilities on January 1, Year 2 are as follows:

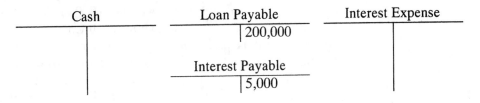

At the end of March, the company pays interest and records two transactions. First, it accrues $5,000 interest expense for the three-month period January through March. Then the company records the $10,000 payment:

Cash	Loan Payable	Interest Expense
	200,000	

	Interest Payable	
	5,000	
	5,000	5,000
10,000	10,000	
	0	

The following is the March transaction in journal entry form with two single entries:

Interest Expense	5,000	
Interest Payable		5,000

Interest Payable	10,000	
Cash		10,000

The compound entry follows:

Interest Expense	5,000	
Interest Payable	5,000	
Cash		10,000

Success with the preceding exercise shows that you understand interest payable. Based on your understanding of this concept, try to work the following interest receivable problem.

Exercise 4-8

Interest Revenue and Interest Receivable. In the previous example, SouthCentral Corporation borrowed $200,000 on April 1 by issuing 10 percent bonds payable. Now we learn that Mitchell Corporation was the lender; it bought all of the bonds. The corporation's interest revenue at 10 percent is $20,000 per year or $10,000 every six months. Mitchell receives cash at the end of March and of September. Mitchell's accountant uses the same numbers as SouthCentral Corporation, the borrower. The initial transfer of cash to SouthCentral Corporation is shown in the following accounts. Show T-account entries to record Mitchell's interest revenue and interest received for the first year.

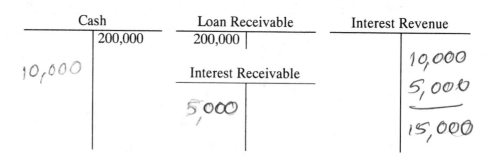

Cash		Loan Receivable		Interest Revenue	
10,000	200,000	200,000			*10,000*
		Interest Receivable			*5,000*
		5,000			*15,000*

Solution

To record the initial receipt of interest at the end of September:

Cash		Loan Receivable		Interest Revenue	
10,000	200,000	200,000			*10,000*
		Interest Receivable			

To record the accrual of three months of interest ($5,000) at the end of December:

Cash		Loan Receivable		Interest Revenue	
10,000	200,000	200,000			10,000
		Interest Receivable			*5,000*
		5,000			*15,000*

Interest revenue for providing services from April 1 to December 31 is $15,000. Since Mitchell receives only $10,000 this year, the interest receivable at the end of the year is $5,000. This corresponds to the borrower's interest payable at the end of Year 1.

Exercise 4-9

Interest Receivable for the Second Year. In continuation of Exercise 4-8, develop and record the transactions for Year 2. Ignore the Loan Receivable account since it does not change during Year 2.

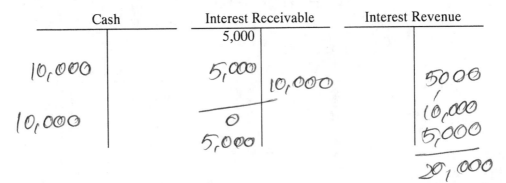

Solution

In March of the second year, Mitchell Corporation records two transactions. First the company records $5,000 interest revenue for the period January through March. Then it records receipt of the $10,000 by debiting Cash and crediting (reducing) the receivable. These transactions are as follows:

Note: The compound entry for March would show a debit to Cash and credits to both Interest Receivable and Interest Revenue.

Cash		Interest Receivable		Interest Revenue	
		5,000			
		5,000			5,000
10,000			10,000		
		0			

In September, Mitchell records $10,000 revenue and the cash receipt. Then, on December 31, the firm reflects the accrual of three months' interest revenue:

Cash		Interest Receivable		Interest Revenue	
		5,000			5,000
		5,000			
10,000			10,000		
		0			
10,000					10,000
		5,000			5,000
					20,000

At this point, Mitchell Corporation's revenue for the year is $20,000 and the ending receivable is $5,000.

**Summary
of key
points**

Recognition of revenue and expense does not always correspond to the timing of cash receipts and payments. Sellers of goods on account record accounts receivable and sales revenue. Buyers in these cases record accounts payable. These receivables and payables are asset and liability accounts. This procedure permits firms to record revenue and purchases before the receipt or payment of cash.

Similar treatments apply to other transactions in which cash collections or payments do not correspond to providing services or receiving services. Examples include receivables and payables for salary, electricity, and interest on borrowed funds.

Appendix to Chapter 4
exercises in financial analysis

These exercises provide additional practice working with concepts discussed in the chapter, introduce basic approaches to financial statement analysis, and help you to relate changes in various accounts with changes in cash. If you have difficulty with any of these exercises, review the topic in the chapter and try again.

Exercise A4-1

Accounts Payable. Businesses record Accounts Payable when they purchase goods on account and reduce Accounts Payable when they make payment. This exercise shows that an understanding of Accounts Payable provides information about other accounts such as Inventory.

In this exercise, the beginning Accounts Payable balance is $70,000. During the year, the company pays $400,000 for inventory and ends with Accounts Payable of $80,000. How much inventory was purchased on account?

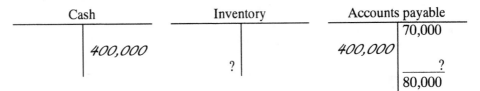

Solution

Inventory purchases were $410,000. Given the beginning and ending accounts payable, we can analyze the situation by first recording the disbursement of cash and reduction of payables. Then we determine the increase to Accounts Payable. This is the cost of inventory purchases.

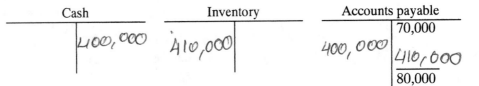

We know that Accounts Payable increase with inventory purchases. Therefore, we can replace the question marks with $410,000, the increase in payables and the amount of purchases.

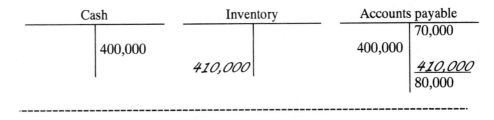

Income isn't always cash

Exercise A4-2

Wages Payable. Wages payable and accounts payable are accounted for in very similar ways. The liability for wages payable increases with wage expense and decreases with payments to workers.

> *Tip: Remember that increases in payables means that the cash payment is less that the expense.*

Quickfreeze Corporation begins and ends the year with the Wages Payable account balances shown in the following T-accounts:

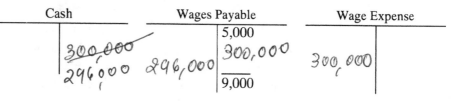

During the year, wage expense was $300,000. How much did Quickfreeze Corporation pay its employees?

Solution

Payments to employees totaled $296,000. The company initially recorded $300,000 as both wage expense and wages payable. It then reduced the liability when it paid the workers.

We started with beginning wages payable of $5,000 and increased this when we recorded the $300,000 expense. Given the $9,000 ending liability, the company must have paid $296,000.

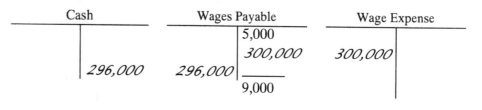

Exercise A4-3

Interest Receivable. This exercise tests your understanding of the Interest Receivable account.

Mastermind Corporation begins the year with $8,000 of Interest Receivable. At the end of the year, the account balance is $10,000. Interest revenue for the year is $80,000. T-accounts are provided to help in your determination of the cash received from borrowers.

Remember that receivables increase with interest revenue and decrease with receipts of cash.

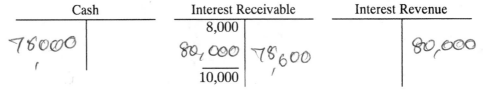

Cash	Interest Receivable	Interest Revenue
78000	8,000	80,000
	80,000 78600	
	10,000	

The cash received from borrowers was

a. $82,000.
b. $78,000.
c. $60,000.
d. $80,000.

Solution

B. The cash received from borrowers was $78,000. Given the $2,000 increase in the receivable, cash receipts are $2,000 less than interest revenue.

The following accounts show that interest receivable and interest revenue both increased by $80,000:

Cash	Interest Receivable	Interest Revenue
78,000	8,000	
	78,000	
	80,000	80,000
	10,000	

Chapter 5

Pay now, expense later
(Costs in advance of expenses)

Costs are amounts paid or to be paid for services. We already know about payments for salaries, utilities, and loans that are recorded immediately as expenses to reflect the use of services. Other payments relate to future accounting periods. For example, tenants sometimes pay their rent in advance. Accountants do not recognize expenses immediately in this case. Instead, they delay the recognition of expenses until the services are used.

This chapter illustrates three important categories of costs in advance: prepayments, long-lived assets, and inventories. Payments for these items occur as required during the year. Expenses, however, are typically entered as adjustments at the end of the accounting period.

Learning objectives

The objectives of this chapter include the following:

- To learn the origin of and transactions relating to prepaid accounts.
- To understand how purchases of long-term assets are recorded.
- To interpret the Accumulated Depreciation account.
- To learn to report depreciation and gains and losses on sale.
- To understand accounting for inventories and the cost of goods sold.

Prepaid rent

Some payments made in advance of the use of services are referred to as prepayments. Examples are prepayments for rent and insurance.

When tenants pay on January 1 for the use of space during the month, they are prepaying their rent. Prepaid rent is recorded as an asset, an item of value. An example follows.

Example

Prepaid Rent. In January our business signs a lease to open a store. The rental is $5,000 per month. Our landlord requires three months payment in advance — $15,000. The entry to record the payment and acquisition of a valuable asset follows:

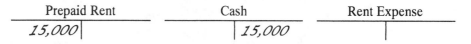

Prepaid Rent	Cash	Rent Expense
15,000	15,000	

Recording the prepayment as an asset rather than as an expense accomplishes two objectives. First, the balance sheet shows an item of value — the right to use the premises for three months. Second, the expense is not recognized until the services are used.

At the end of the first month, the use of services is recorded as follows:

Prepaid Rent		Cash		Rent Expense	
15,000			15,000		
	5,000			*5,000*	
10,000					

Note that the prepaid rent balance decreases to $10,000 after one month.

The accounts show that at this point classification of the $15,000 payment is divided. Part of the payment shows as rent expense and the remainder shows as an asset, prepaid rent.

This procedure continues for the second and third months until the entire prepaid rent balance is expensed. (In practice, rental agreements usually provide for prepaid rent balances to be maintained at all times. Thus, a second cash payment and an addition to prepaid rent will probably be required at the end of the first month.)

Exercise 5-1

Prepaid Rent. The preceding example considers the $15,000 advance payment of rent. This reflects rental costs of $5,000 per month for three months. After one month, the Prepaid Rent account balance is $10,000. Assuming no additional payments, use the following T-accounts and record entries for the next two months.

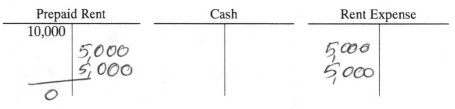

Prepaid Rent		Cash		Rent Expense	
10,000					
	5,000			*5,000*	
	5,000			*5,000*	
0					

Solution

Beginning with the $10,000 Prepaid Rent account balance, the company expenses an additional $5,000 per month until the Prepaid Rent account balance is reduced to zero. Your T-account entries should look like the following:

Prepaid Rent		Cash		Rent Expense	
10,000					
	5,000			*5,000*	
	5,000			*5,000*	
0					

Note that over the three-month period, the expense totals $15,000. This is the same as the cash payment. Over the long run, the cash paid for services always becomes an expense.

Prepaid insurance

Insurance companies usually require policyholders to pay premiums in advance. The payments are initially recorded as Prepaid Insurance, an asset. This asset is then reduced gradually as time passes and the insurance provides protection. Accounting for prepaid insurance and rent follow the same procedure. If you understand how to account for prepaid rent, you should be able to account for prepaid insurance.

Exercise 5-2

Prepaid Insurance. Carson Company purchases an insurance policy for $12,000 on January 1. The policy provides for a full year of liability insurance. On January 1 the entry is as follows:

Prepaid Insurance	Cash	Insurance Expense
12,000	12,000	

Record the transactions to adjust the accounts at the ends of January and February. Then show the Prepaid Insurance account balance at the end of two months.

Prepaid Insurance	Cash	Insurance Expense
12,000	12,000	
_1000_		_1000_
_1000_		_1,000_
_10,000_		

Solution

Insurance expense is $1,000 per month ($12,000 annual / 12 months). Over the two-month period, prepaid insurance decreases from $12,000 to $10,000 as follows:

Prepaid Insurance	Cash	Insurance Expense
12,000	12,000	
1,000		1,000
1,000		1,000
10,000		

Exercise 5-3

Prepaid Insurance. Waterville Corporation renews its one-year insurance policy at the beginning of July. The policy amount is $60,000 with the entire amount payable in advance on July 1. Show all entries for July, August, and September.

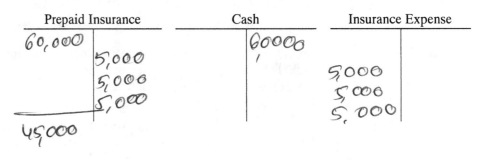

Prepaid Insurance		Cash		Insurance Expense	
60,000	5,000	60000			5000
	5,000				5,000
	5,000				5,000
45,000					

Solution

Since the 12-month policy is for $60,000, insurance expense will be $5,000 per month. The accounts should show this information:

Prepaid Insurance		Cash		Insurance Expense	
60,000		60,000			
	5,000			5,000	
	5,000			5,000	
	5,000			5,000	
45,000					

The $45,000 ending Prepaid Insurance account balance provides for nine more months of service at $5,000 per month. At the end of 12 months, the expense at $5,000 per month will total $60,000. The cumulative expense must equal the $60,000 payment.

Exercise 5-4

Prepaid Accounts. Frame Corporation begins the year with $12,000 in prepaid insurance. During the year, Frame pays an additional $50,000 for insurance. Insurance expense during the year is $60,000. What is the ending balance in the Prepaid Insurance account?

Tip: We know that prepaid asset accounts increase with payments and decrease with expenses, the use of services.

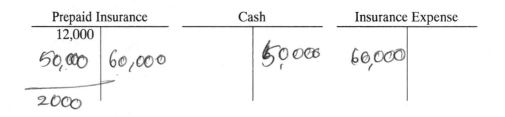

Prepaid Insurance		Cash		Insurance Expense	
12,000					
50,000	60,000	50,000		60,000	
2000					

Solution
The ending Prepaid Insurance account balance is $2,000. This account increases by the $50,000 payment and decreases by the $60,000 expense as shown in the following entries:

Prepaid Insurance		Cash		Insurance Expense	
12,000					
50,000		50,000			
_____	60,000			60,000	
2,000					

Since prepaid insurance reflects payments to the insurance company, we increase the Prepaid Insurance account when we make the $50,000 payment. Then we decrease this account over time as we benefit from the insurance. In this case, the use of services is given as $60,000. A compound entry leads to the same result. Prepaid insurance decreases by $10,000 because payments for the year are less than the $60,000 amount of insurance services used.

Prepaid Insurance		Cash		Insurance Expense	
12,000					
_____	10,000	50,000		60,000	
2,000					

Long-lived assets

Long-lived assets represent a second important category of costs in advance of expenses. When a company acquires property with a long expected life, it records the initial cost as an asset. It records expenses later through a process called depreciation. Depreciation is just an allocation process that records expense gradually over the period of expected benefit.

Example

Depreciation Expense. Jones Network Company purchases a building for $200,000. This building has an expected life of 20 years.

Initially, the $200,000 cost is recorded as an asset. The expense is recorded later as depreciation. Accountants usually calculate depreciation expense by apportioning the asset's cost over its expected life as follows:

Annual Depreciation Expense = Amount to Be Depreciated / Expected Life

= $200,000 / 20 years

= $10,000 per year

Depreciation reduces income and the asset balance (as the asset is considered to be used). Accountants show the reduction in the asset in a separate account called Accumulated Depreciation.

Accumulated depreciation

Accumulated depreciation is the cumulative depreciation recorded since the asset was acquired. An example follows.

Example

The Accumulated Depreciation Account. Bristol Company purchases a $400,000 building with an expected life of 20 years. Entries to record the purchase and the first year's depreciation expense follow:

Building	Cash	Depreciation Expense
400,000	400,000	

Accumulated Depreciation		
20,000		20,000

Bristol records an asset when it buys the building. Then the business makes an adjusting entry to record the $20,000 expense and credit to Accumulated Depreciation. When depreciation expense is recorded, an equal amount is credited to Accumulated Depreciation.

Comparison of the differences between the balances in the Building and Accumulated Depreciation accounts indicates a net amount of $380,000. This is referred to as book value or carrying value. Some accountants also refer to the building, net. We'll refer to the net amount as book value.

Building	$400,000
Accumulated depreciation	20,000
Book value	$380,000

Note that the Accumulated Depreciation account always has a right-side balance.

Accumulated Depreciation is called a contra account because the balance is opposite that of the long-lived asset account. Accumulated depreciation has a right-side balance while the primary account, the building, has a left-side balance. Both accounts are permanent accounts.

The Accumulated Depreciation account balance increases each year with each year's depreciation expense. Accumulated depreciation, however, will never exceed the balance in the Building or other primary account. Depreciation, as indicated earlier, simply assigns the expected cost of ownership over the period of expected benefit. Once this occurs, depreciation is no longer recorded.

Exercise 5-5
Accumulated Depreciation. The following accounts show balances for Bristol Company's Building and Accumulated Depreciation accounts at the end of Year 1. Depreciation expense is $20,000 each year. Show the Year 2 and 3 entries to Depreciation Expense and Accumulated Depreciation. Then calculate the building's book value at the end of Year 3.

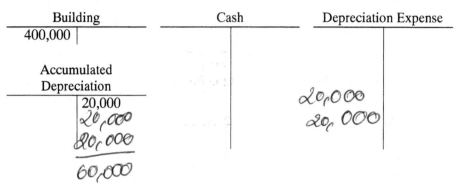

Building		Cash		Depreciation Expense
400,000				
Accumulated				
Depreciation				
	20,000			20,000
	20,000			20,000
	20,000			
	60,000			

Solution
The building's book value at the end of Year 3 is $340,000. Accumulated depreciation increases at the rate of $20,000 per year. At the end of Year 3, the Accumulated Depreciation account balance is $60,000. The book value, then, must be $340,000 ($400,000 - $60,000). The entries in Year 2 and Year 3 to record depreciation expense and accumulated depreciation follow:

Building		Cash		Depreciation Expense
400,000				
Accumulated				
Depreciation				
	20,000			
	20,000			20,000
	20,000			20,000
	60,000			

Note that accumulated depreciation may not exceed the asset's original cost.

After 17 more years, accumulated depreciation will be $400,000. Then depreciation stops because the building is fully depreciated.

Exercise 5-6
Depreciation Expense and Accumulated Depreciation. Accelerated Computer Company buys new equipment with a 10-year expected life for $80,000. Determine the annual depreciation expense and the equipment's book value at the end of Year 5. The following relationship and T-accounts should be helpful:

Annual Depreciation Expense = Amount to Be Depreciated / Expected Life

$$= 80000 / 10 = 8000 \text{ per year}$$

Equipment	Cash	Depreciation Expense
80,000		

Accumulated Depreciation		
8,000		8000
8,000		8,000
8,000		8,000
8,000		8,000
8,000		8,000
40,000		

Solution

The annual depreciation expense is $8,000, and the book value at the end of Year 5 is $40,000. We calculate depreciation using the following relationship:

Annual Depreciation Expense = Amount to Be Depreciated / Expected Life

$$= \$80,000 / 10 \text{ years} = \$8,000 \text{ per year}$$

Entries to record depreciation expense and accumulated depreciation follow:

Equipment	Cash	Depreciation Expense
80,000		

Accumulated Depreciation		
8,000		8,000
8,000		8,000
8,000		8,000
8,000		8,000
8,000		8,000
40,000		

The equipment's book value is the amount in the Equipment account less the amount in the Accumulated Depreciation account as follows:

Equipment	$80,000
Accumulated depreciation	40,000
Book value	$40,000

Sale of long-lived assets

When businesses sell property for cash, the sellers record the cash and remove the property from the books. Initially, we consider the purchase and sale of land which is not depreciated because, unlike trucks or machines, it doesn't ordinarily lose its usefulness.

Example

Purchase and Sale of Land. Lilien Corporation purchases land for $500,000 to build a small shopping plaza. Several years later, Lilien decides not to build and sells the land for $500,000. The purchase is recorded as follows:

Land	*500,000*	
Cash		*500,000*

When the land is sold for $500,000 this entry is then reversed.

Cash	*500,000*	
Land		*500,000*

The T-account form follows:

Land			Cash	
500,000				*500,000*
	500,000		*500,000*	

Gains on sale

In practice, it isn't usual to buy and sell assets at the same price because their values change over time. This leads to gains or losses on sale. <u>Gains</u> are recorded when selling prices exceed book values. <u>Losses</u> mean that selling prices are less than book values.

Example

Gains on Sale. Colorado Corporation purchases land for $800,000 on which it plans to expand its factory. Three years later, the company closes the factory and sells the land for $850,000. Colorado recognizes a $50,000 gain on sale. This gain is the difference between the selling price and book value, as shown in the following accounts:

Land			Cash			Gain on Sale	
800,000							
	800,000		*850,000*				*50,000*
0							

The journal entry form follows:

Cash	*850,000*	
Land		*800,000*
Gain on Sale		*50,000*

The interpretation of gains and losses on sale

Gains and losses increase or decrease income. In this respect, they resemble revenues and expenses. Income statements, however, report gains and losses separately because they are usually one-time items. For example, when a store records revenue, it ordinarily expects similar revenue in the future. This is not the case for gains on sale. Once the business sells land, investments, or equipment, the items are gone. There will be no future gains on sale from these particular items. In fact, it isn't unusual for a company to report gains in one year and losses in the following year. The following income statement shows a typical presentation of a gain on sale.

Colorado Corporation
Income for the year ended December 31, 20x1

Sales Revenue		$400,000
Expenses		
Cost of Goods Sold	$300,000	
Other Expenses	70,000	370,000
Income From Operations		$ 30,000
Gain on Sale of Equipment		50,000
Income Before Taxes		$ 80,000

Gains and losses are closed to Income Summary using the same procedure applicable to revenues and expenses.

Exercise 5-7

Tip: The loss on sale is the difference between the book value and the selling price.

Loss on Sale. Secure Corporation purchased land for $400,000 and then sold the property for $310,000. Determine the loss on sale and show T-accounts for the purchase and sale transactions.

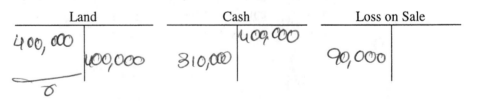

Solution

Since the selling price is $90,000 less than book value, Secure Corporation shows a loss on sale. The entries to record the purchase and sale follow:

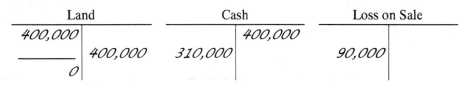

Land		Cash		Loss on Sale	
400,000			400,000		
	400,000	310,000		90,000	
	0				

In the sale transaction, the Land account is reduced by the land's original cost. This is necessary since the company no longer has the property. Cash increases by the $310,000 selling price. The loss is the difference between the selling price and the book value — $400,000 less $310,000. In journal entry form, the transaction is as follows:

Cash	310,000	
Loss on Sale	90,000	
Land		400,000

Tip: Losses reduce owners' equity.	How can we be sure that the $90,000 amount is a loss rather than a gain? The loss account has a left-side entry that reduces equity. Mechanically, losses work the same way as expenses, but the interpretation differs because losses on sale are one-time occurrences.

The sale of depreciable property

We now consider the sale of depreciable property. The same principles apply to the sale of land and depreciable property. With depreciable property, however, an additional account is involved. When equipment or other depreciable property is sold, accountants close both the asset and associated Accumulated Depreciation accounts.

Exercise 5-8

Review of Accounting for Depreciable Property. Santel Corporation pays $100,000 for equipment with an expected life of five years. Santel continues to use the equipment during Year 6. Depreciation stops, however, after five years. At this point, the Accumulated Depreciation account balance equals the cost of the equipment. This review exercise involves entries to record depreciation expense. Use the following T-accounts:

Equipment	
100,000	

Cash	
	100,000

Depreciation Expense	
20,000	
20,000	
20,000	
20,000	
20,000	

Accumulated Depreciation	
	20,000
	20,000
	20,000
	20,000
	20,000
	100,000

Solution

Entries for the six-year period are as follows:

Equipment	
100,000	

Cash	
	100,000

Depreciation Expense	
20,000	
20,000	
20,000	
20,000	
20,000	

Accumulated Depreciation	
	20,000
	20,000
	20,000
	20,000
	20,000
	100,000

At the end of Year 5, the equipment's book value is zero. The equipment is now fully depreciated and, consequently, it is not possible to record additional depreciation expense in Year 6.

Depreciation and cash

Note that in the previous exercises, we did not record any entries to Cash when we depreciated the equipment. This illustrates an important concept. Depreciation is purely an allocation of previously recorded costs. It may be an important determinant of income, but depreciation has absolutely no impact on the Cash account.

Exercise 5-9   **Gain or Loss on Sale**. In the previous review exercise, Santel Corporation bought equipment for $100,000 and depreciated it to zero book value over five years. Now we learn that the corporation sells the equipment early in Year 7 for $35,000. Calculate the gain on sale by comparing the $35,000 cash received on sale to the Year 7 book value. Then record the entry for the sale. Be sure to remove the Accumulated Depreciation account from the books when you remove the Equipment account.

Obtain the gain by comparing the selling price to the book value:

Selling price	35,000
Book value	0
Gain on sale	35,000

The journal entry follows:

Cash	35,000	
Accumulated Depreciation	100,000	
Equipment		100,000
Gain on Sale		35,000

Starting with the balances that follow, update T-accounts for Year 7 by recording the information in the preceding journal entry.

Equipment	Cash	Gain on Sale
100,000 100,000	100,000	
0		
		35,000
Accumulated Depreciation	35000	
100,000		
100,000		
0		

Solution   Santel Corporation calculates a $35,000 gain as follows:

Selling price	$35,000
Book value	0
Gain on sale	$35,000

Pay now, expense later

The company then makes the following journal entry:

Cash	*35,000*	
Accumulated Depreciation	*100,000*	
Equipment		*100,000*
Gain on Sale		*35,000*

Santel debits Cash to show the receipt of a valuable asset. The company also debits Accumulated Depreciation to offset the amount shown in this contra account. (We can't show an amount for Accumulated Depreciation on the books if we no longer have the item.) Then we remove the asset from the books with a credit to the Equipment account. The gain can be calculated as the missing number necessary to ensure that debits equal credits.

The Year 7 T-account entries are as follows:

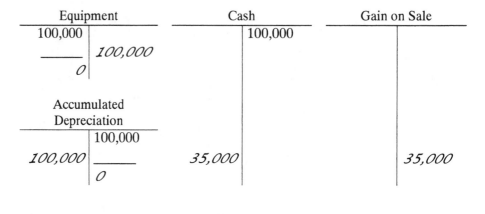

When the book value is not zero

If the book value is not zero at the time of sale, the gain differs from the selling price. The next exercise assumes that the property is sold before it is fully depreciated.

Exercise 5-10

Accounting for Depreciable Property. Santel Corporation buys equipment costing $100,000 and begins to depreciate the property over five years. Early in Year 4, before depreciation is recorded, Santel sells the equipment for $110,000.

First calculate the book value at the time of sale. To do this, refer to entries up to the time of sale as follows. Then determine the gain on sale and record the entry for the sale.

Equipment	Cash	Depreciation Expense
100,000	100,000	

Accumulated Depreciation		
20,000		20,000
20,000		20,000
20,000		20,000
60,000		

The following is the journal entry to record the sale:

Cash		*110,000*
Accumulated Depreciation		*60,000*
Equipment		*100,000*
Gain on Sale		*70,000*

Starting with the balances shown here, update the T-accounts for Year 4.

Equipment	Cash	Gain on Sale
100,000	*100,000*	100,000	*70,000*
0		

Accumulated Depreciation		Depreciation Expense
20,000	*110,000*	20,000
20,000		20,000
20,000		20,000
60,000		
60,000		
0		

Solution   In this case, Santel calculates a $70,000 gain as follows:

Selling price	$110,000
Book value	40,000
Gain on sale	$ 70,000

The company shows a $110,000 debit to record the receipt of cash. It also debits Accumulated Depreciation for $60,000, the amount on the books at the time of sale. Crediting Equipment for its $100,000 cost removes this account from the books. The gain can also be determined as the missing number necessary to complete the following entry:

Cash	*110,000*	
Accumulated Depreciation	*60,000*	
Equipment		*100,000*
Gain on Sale		*70,000*

Santel's T-accounts show the following:

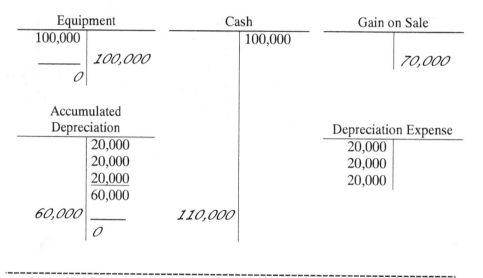

Exercise 5-11

Loss on the Sale of Depreciable Property. Sparkle Corporation buys a new truck for $300,000 and begins to depreciate the property over three years. Early in Year 3, Sparkle sells the truck for $70,000.

First calculate the annual depreciation and record depreciation expense in the following T-accounts for two years (to the beginning of Year 3). Then determine the loss on sale. Finally, record the entry for the sale.

Annual Depreciation Expense = Amount to Be Depreciated / Expected Life

$$= 300,000 / 3$$

$$= 100,000 \text{ per year}$$

The T-account entries for the first two years follow:

Truck		Cash		Loss on Sale
300,000	*300,000*		300,000	*30,000*
0		*70,000*		

Accumulated Depreciation		Depreciation Expense
	100,000	*100,000*
200,000	*100,000*	*100,000*
	0	

Find the loss by comparing the selling price and book value.

Selling price	*70,000*
Book value	*100,000*
Loss on sale	*30,000*

The entry to record the sale follows:

Cash	*70000*	
Accumulated Depreciation	*200,000*	
Loss on sale	*30,000*	
Truck		*300,000*

Solution Sparkle has a $30,000 loss on sale because the selling price is less than the truck's book value.

Annual Depreciation Expense = Amount to Be Depreciated / Expected Life

= $300,000 / 3 years

= $100,000 per year

After two years, Sparkle's accumulated depreciation is $200,000 and the book value is reduced to $100,000. This leads to a loss on sale as follows:

Selling price	$ 70,000
Book value	100,000
Loss on sale	$ 30,000

The journal entry to record the sale follows:

Cash	70,000	
Accumulated Depreciation	200,000	
Loss on Sale	30,000	
Truck		300,000

Sparkle makes the following T-account entries for Years 1 and 2:

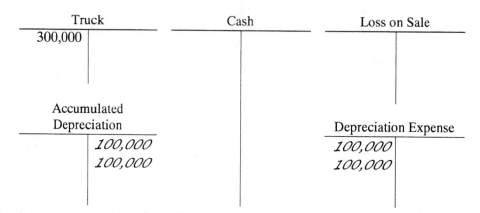

The Year 3 entry to record the sale follows:

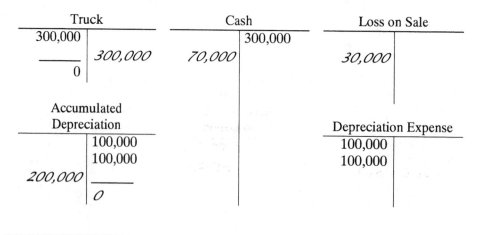

Residual value

Residual value is the amount received when the asset is sold; it is also called salvage value. Accountants always estimate expected residual value. If we buy property for $500,000 and expect to sell it for $200,000, the expected residual value is $200,000. In this case, the expected net cost of ownership is only $300,000 ($500,000 purchase price less $200,000 expected selling price). Only the expected net cost is subject to depreciation. We'll see that this approach always reduces income in the long run by the net cost of owning the property.

Example

Depreciable Property with Residual Value. Sicily Corporation pays $200,000 for a computer. Its expected life is three years and its expected residual value (future selling price) is $20,000. During Year 4, Sicily sells the computer for $30,000.

Since the cost will be partially offset by the $20,000 estimated residual value, the expected net cost of ownership is only $180,000 ($200,000 - $20,000). We depreciate this amount.

Annual Depreciation Expense = Amount to Be Depreciated / Expected Life

= (Cost - Residual Value) / Expected Life

= ($200,000 - $20,000) / 3 years

= $60,000 per year

With annual depreciation of $60,000, accumulated depreciation totals $180,000 after three years. The book value then will be $20,000 (equal to the expected selling price). Thus, a sale at exactly $20,000 will not result in gain or loss. The following T-accounts show the transactions to the time of sale:

Computer	Cash	Gain/ Loss on Sale
200,000	*200,000*	

Accumulated Depreciation	Depreciation Expense
60,000	*60,000*
60,000	*60,000*
60,000	*60,000*
180,000	

Note that accumulated depreciation may not exceed the asset's original cost.

At the time of sale, the journal entry is as follows:

Cash	*20,000*	
Accumulated Depreciation	*180,000*	
Computer		*200,000*

In T-account form, the sale is shown as follows:

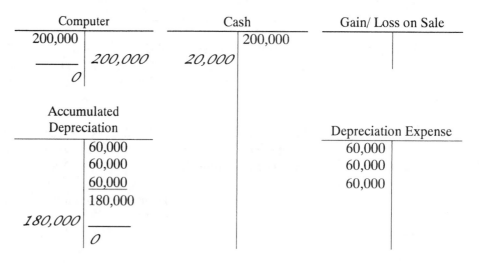

Computer		Cash		Gain/ Loss on Sale
200,000			200,000	
	200,000	20,000		
0				

Accumulated Depreciation				Depreciation Expense
	60,000			60,000
	60,000			60,000
	60,000			60,000
	180,000			
180,000				
	0			

Since Sicily Corporation paid $200,000 for the computer and later sold it for $20,000, the net cost of ownership is $180,000. This must equal the $180,000 cumulative depreciation expense.

Exercise 5-12

Tip: Since the residual value is $20,000, only $100,000 of the cost will be depreciated.

Depreciable Property with Residual Value and a Gain on Sale. Venture Company pays $120,000 for a new machine that has a four-year expected life and a $20,000 expected residual value. Venture sells the machine for $58,000 early in Year 3.

Calculate the annual depreciation and then record depreciation entries for two years. Finally, record the sale for Year 3.

Annual Depreciation Expense = Amount to Be Depreciated / Expected Life

= (Cost - Residual Value) / Expected Life

$= (120,000 - 20000) / 4$

$= 25,000$

The following are the T-account entries for the first two years:

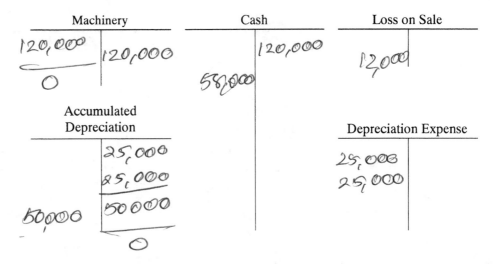

At the time of sale, the journal entry is as follows:

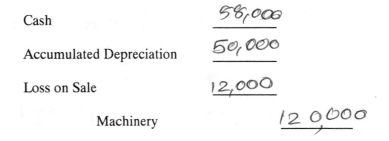

Cash	58,000
Accumulated Depreciation	50,000
Loss on Sale	12,000
Machinery	120,000

Solution

Venture Company records a $12,000 loss on sale.

Annual Depreciation Expense = Amount to Be Depreciated / Expected Life

= (Cost - Residual Value) / Expected Life

= ($120,000 - $20,000) / 4 years

= $25,000 per year

T-account entries for the first two years are as follows:

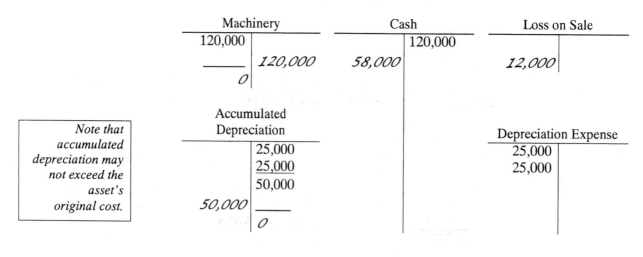

Machinery		Cash		Loss on Sale
120,000			120,000	

Accumulated Depreciation		Depreciation Expense
	25,000	25,000
	25,000	25,000
	50,000	

At the time of sale, the journal entry is the following:

Cash	58,000	
Accumulated Depreciation	50,000	
Loss on Sale	12,000	
Machinery		120,000

In T-account form, the sale is recorded as follows:

Machinery		Cash		Loss on Sale
120,000			120,000	
_____	120,000	58,000		12,000
	0			

Note that accumulated depreciation may not exceed the asset's original cost.

Accumulated Depreciation		Depreciation Expense
	25,000	25,000
	25,000	25,000
	50,000	
50,000	_____	
	0	

Inventory   Inventory is a third important cost in advance of expense. In some respects, this is a review since inventory was discussed earlier in the basic transactions exercises. You learned that the costs of items manufactured or purchased for resale are recorded as assets. Inventory is reduced and expenses are recorded as the goods are sold. The cost of goods sold is recognized at the time of sale because this is when the ownership of inventory transfers to the buyer. Services are assumed to be used at this time.

Example   **Inventory**. PTech Corporation buys 100 computers for $2,500 each. During the year, it sells 80 of these items to customers. This means that 20 computers remain in inventory at year-end. The entry to record purchases follows:

Inventory	Accounts Payable	Cost of Goods Sold
250,000	*250,000*	

PTech now has 100 items available for sale at a cost of $250,000. For accounting purposes, the cost of goods available breaks into two components: ending inventory and the cost of goods sold.

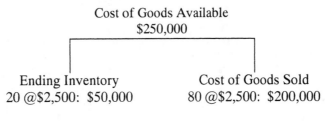

Cost of Goods Available
$250,000

Ending Inventory   Cost of Goods Sold
20 @$2,500: $50,000   80 @$2,500: $200,000

Remember that for accounting purposes only two conditions are possible: The business either still has the item or has sold it.

Since 80 percent of the computers are sold, 80 percent of the original purchase price is expensed. The remaining $50,000 will be expensed when all computers are sold. The entry to adjust the inventory and record the cost of goods sold as follows:

Inventory	Accounts Payable	Cost of Goods Sold
250,000	250,000	
_____ *200,000*		*200,000*
50,000		

After the first year in business, the cost of goods available consists of beginning inventory plus the cost of purchases. The next exercise considers the usual ongoing inventory situation.

Exercise 5-13

Inventory and the Cost of Goods Sold. Forester Company, a large pet store, begins the year with 100 puppies each costing $20. During the year, the company buys 1,000 additional puppies for $20 each. This means that 1,100 puppies are available for sale. Of the 1,100 puppies available for sale, 1,050 are sold during the year.

Your challenge is to find the cost of goods available. Then determine the cost of ending inventory and the cost of goods sold. Finally, make the appropriate entries in the T-accounts.

First determine the cost of goods available for sale.

	Number of Puppies	Total Cost
Beginning Inventory	100	2,000
Purchases	1,000	20,000
Cost of Goods Available	1,100	22,000

Then divide the cost of goods available into its components.

Cost of Goods Available

Ending Inventory
$50 \times 20 = 1000$

Cost of Goods Sold
$1050 \times 20 = 21,000$

Finally record entries for the purchase and sale of inventory.

Inventory	Accounts Payable	Cost of Goods Sold
2,000		
20,000	20,000	21,000
21,000		
1000		

Solution

The cost of goods available for sale is as follows:

	Number of Puppies	Total Cost
Beginning Inventory	100 @ $20	$ 2,000
Purchases	1,000 @ $20	20,000
Cost of Goods Available	1,100 @ $20	$22,000

The following are the components of the cost of goods available:

Cost of Goods Available
$22,000

Ending Inventory
50 @$20: $1,000

Cost of Goods Sold
1,050 @$20: $21,000

In T-account form the accounts are as follows:

Inventory	Accounts Payable	Cost of Goods Sold
2,000		
20,000	20,000	
	21,000	21,000
21,000		
1,000		

The following exercise is similar to the previous one. You may wish to skip it if you're comfortable with the Forester Company exercise.

Exercise 5-14

Tip: Always begin with the cost of goods available for sale.

Inventories and the Cost of Goods Sold. Fastrack, Incorporated, sells a number of products including tennis rackets. The company begins the year with 125 rackets costing $100 each. During the year, Fastrack buys 500 rackets at the same price. At the end of the year, only 25 rackets remain in inventory. Calculate the cost of goods sold and cost of ending inventory, and record these entries in the accounts.

	Number of Items	Total Cost
Beginning Inventory	125	12,500
Purchases	500	50,000
Cost of Goods Available	625	62,500

Divide the cost of goods available into its components.

Cost of Goods Available

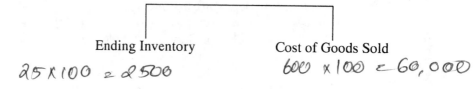

Ending Inventory   Cost of Goods Sold

25 X 100 = 2500   *600 x 100 = 60,000*

After this, record entries for the purchase and sale of inventory.

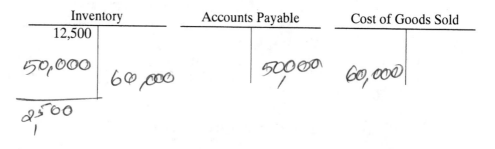

Inventory		Accounts Payable	Cost of Goods Sold
12,500			
50,000	*60,000*	*50000*	*60,000*
2500			

Solution

The cost of goods available for sale is as follows:

	Number of Items	Total Cost
Beginning Inventory	125 @ $100	$12,500
Purchases	500 @ $100	50,000
Cost of Goods Available	625 @ $100	$62,500

The following are the components of the cost of goods available:

Cost of Goods Available
$62,500

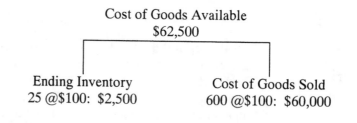

Ending Inventory   Cost of Goods Sold
25 @$100: $2,500   600 @$100: $60,000

This can also be worked using T-accounts:

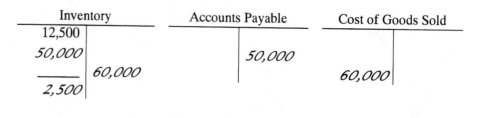

Inventory		Accounts Payable	Cost of Goods Sold
12,500			
50,000		50,000	
———	60,000		60,000
2,500			

Summary

Prepayments

Prepaid assets are recorded in the accounts when businesses pay for services before the services are actually received. This accounting procedure serves two purposes. First, the balance sheet shows an item of value — the right to use services in the future. Second, the expense is recognized when the services are used. With any prepayment situation, the amount paid eventually becomes an expense.

Long-lived assets

Property with a long expected life is initially recorded as an asset. The expense, which comes later, is called depreciation.

Depreciation is an allocation process that provides for recording expense gradually over the period of expected benefit. Over the long run, depreciation expense should equal the net cost of ownership. Depreciation expense reduces income and the book value of assets. Depreciation expense, however, does not reduce cash.

Accumulated depreciation

The reduction in the book value of the asset is shown separately in an account called Accumulated Depreciation. This account increases each year with cumulative depreciation expense. Accumulated Depreciation is called a contra account because the balance is opposite to that of the primary account. Comparison of the differences between the balances in the asset and Accumulated Depreciation accounts gives a net amount referred to as book value or carrying value.

Asset sales

When property is sold for cash, the seller records cash and removes the item from the books. Property sales usually result in gains or losses. These are temporary accounts that are closed to Income Summary. Both the asset and Accumulated Depreciation accounts must be removed from the books when depreciable property is sold.

Residual value is the amount received when the asset is sold. Only the cost less residual value is subject to depreciation. This approach always reduces income in the long run by the net cost of ownership.

Inventory

Inventory purchases are not expensed until the time of sale, which is when the use of services occurs. The cost of goods available for sale is the cost of beginning inventory plus the cost of additional purchases. It has two components: the cost of ending inventory and the cost of goods sold.

Appendix to Chapter 5
exercises in financial analysis

Prepay-ments

This group of exercises involves prepayments, long-lived assets, and inventory relationships. The first group of exercises provides practice working with changes in prepaid accounts.

Exercise A5-1

Prepaid Accounts. This exercise provides practice in working with changes in prepaid accounts to determine the amount paid for new insurance. Investors, lenders, and other financial statement users are concerned about cash because it repays loans and pays dividends on investments. Understanding which events increase and decrease account balances permits you to determine cash paid for insurance and other items that are not disclosed in the financial statements.

Health Corporation begins the year with $22,000 in prepaid insurance. During the year, insurance expense is $100,000 and the ending Prepaid Insurance account balance is $32,000. How much was paid for insurance this year?

Tip: We know that payments reduce prepaid accounts.

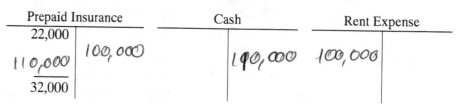

Prepaid Insurance		Cash	Rent Expense
22,000			
110,000	100,000	190,000 100,000	
32,000			

Solution

Payments for insurance were $110,000. The key to this problem is understanding that prepaid asset accounts increase with payments and decrease with expenses. We know that the Prepaid Insurance account was reduced by $100,000 and that the ending balance is $32,000. The challenge is to solve for the question marks.

Prepaid Insurance		Cash	Rent Expense
22,000			
?	100,000	?	100,000
32,000			

The corporation must have added $110,000 to Prepaid Insurance. It began the year with $22,000 in prepaid insurance and during the year paid $110,000 to the insurance company and used services worth $100,000. This leaves the ending Prepaid Insurance account balance at $32,000, as shown in the following accounts:

Prepaid Insurance		Cash		Rent Expense	
22,000					
	100,000			100,000	
_110,000_		_110,000_			
32,000					

Exercise A5-2

Prepaid Accounts. This exercise is similar to the previous one. Trail Corporation begins the year with $15,000 in prepaid insurance. During the year, the company pays $90,000 to the insurance company and the ending Prepaid Insurance account balance is $5,000. What is the insurance expense for the year?

Tip: Remember that prepaid accounts increase with payments and decrease with the expense.

Prepaid Insurance		Cash		Rent Expense	
15,000			90,000		100,000
90,000	100,000				
5,000					

Solution

Insurance expense is $100,000. Some of the beginning prepaid insurance was used. Therefore, the expense exceeded the $90,000 amount paid.

Given that the Prepaid Insurance account initially increased by $90,000 (the payments) and the ending balance is $5,000, the expense must be $100,000. Put differently, the only way to start with the $15,000 Prepaid Insurance account balance, pay $90,000 for insurance, and end with Prepaid Insurance of $5,000, is to incur insurance expense of $100,000. The following accounts show the $90,000 addition to Prepaid Insurance (the payment) and the $100,000 reduction for insurance expense:

Prepaid Insurance		Cash		Rent Expense	
15,000					
90,000		90,000			
	100,000			100,000	.
5,000					

Long-lived assets

This group of exercises provides practice with long-lived asset and Accumulated Depreciation account relationships. It also shows how analysts can use asset and Accumulated Depreciation account relationships to develop information not provided directly in the accounts.

Exercise A5-3

Tip: Remember that accumulated depreciation increases with depreciation expense.

Equipment and Accumulated Depreciation Account Relationships. The Equipment account increases with purchases and decreases when the equipment is sold. Accumulated depreciation increases with depreciation expense. When old equipment is sold, the accumulated depreciation to date is removed from the Accumulated Depreciation account. The first exercise is a warm-up in that it involves only two trucks.

Wind Company begins the year with one delivery truck. During the year, the depreciation expense recorded for the truck is $6,000. At the end of the year, Wind sells the truck and recognizes a gain on sale of $4,000. Then the company buys a new truck. The following T-accounts show the beginning and ending balances for the Truck and Accumulated Depreciation accounts. Our challenge is to calculate the amount received on the sale of the old truck and the cost of the new truck.

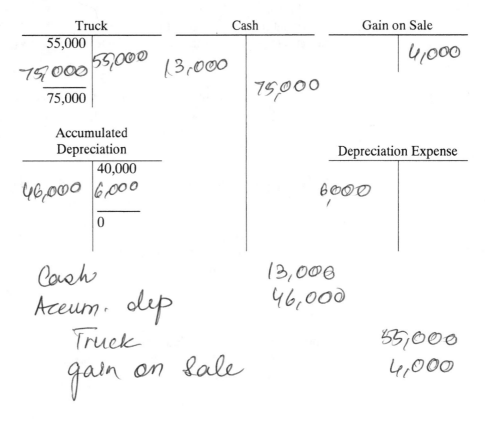

Solution

The cash received from the sale of the old truck was $13,000. The new truck cost $75,000. First, record the depreciation expense as follows:

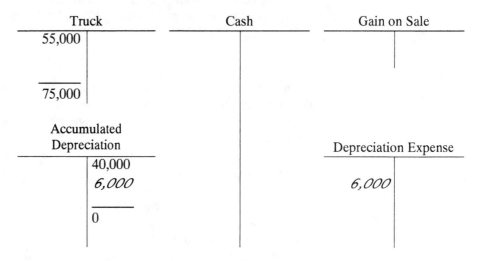

Additional depreciation expense brings the Accumulated Depreciation account balance to $46,000. We know that Accumulated Depreciation must be reduced by $46,000 to bring the account balance to zero when the truck is sold. We also know that the Truck account must be reduced to zero. The entry to record the sale has four parts. Of these, we know three as follows:

Cash	*?*	
Accumulated Depreciation	*46,000*	
Truck		*55,000*
Gain on Sale		*4,000*

Given the preceding analysis, the cash received on the sale must have been $13,000. This is necessary for debits to equal credits.

Cash	*13,000*	
Accumulated Depreciation	*46,000*	
Truck		*55,000*
Gain on Sale		*4,000*

Another approach is to calculate the old truck's book value. Comparing the $55,000 cost and $46,000 accumulated depreciation gives a $9,000 book value. Then the selling price has to be $13,000 to provide a $4,000 gain on sale.

Selling price	$13,000
Book value	9,000
Gain on Sale	$ 4,000

We know the company paid $75,000 for the new truck because this is the only way that the Truck account can show a $75,000 ending balance. (The company debited the Truck account and credited Cash when it purchased the new truck for $75,000.) T-account entries to reflect the sale of the old truck and the purchase of the new truck are as follows:

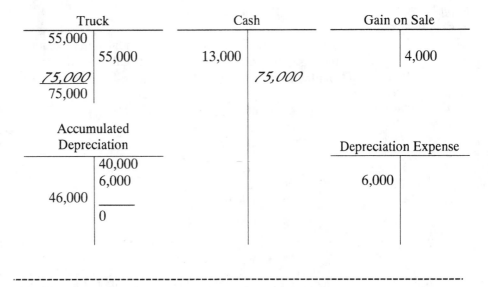

Truck		Cash		Gain on Sale	
55,000					
	55,000	13,000			4,000
_75,000_			_75,000_		
75,000					

Accumulated Depreciation				Depreciation Expense	
	40,000				
	6,000			6,000	
46,000	____				
	0				

Exercise A5-4

Hint: T-accounts can be very helpful with this type of problem.

Hint: Accumulated depreciation decreases by the depreciation accumulated on items sold during the year.

Accumulated Depreciation. Foster Corporation's Accumulated Depreciation account began the year with a $50,000 balance and ended with a $60,000 balance. Depreciation expense for the year was $230,000. Foster sold long-lived assets during the year. How much depreciation was accumulated on the items that the company sold?

Since we know the beginning accumulated depreciation and the amount of the increase, the primary challenge is to calculate the entry to Accumulated Depreciation made on the sale of long-lived assets.

Accumulated Depreciation		Depreciation Expense
	50,000	
220,000	*230,000*	*230,000*
	60,000	

Solution

The accumulated depreciation applicable to the equipment sold was $220,000. This is the most likely cause of the change in the Accumulated Depreciation account balance. Substituting in the following set of accounts demonstrates that reducing Accumulated Depreciation by $220,000 provides the $60,000 ending Accumulated Depreciation account balance.

Accumulated Depreciation		Depreciation Expense
	50,000	
	230,000	230,000
220,000		
	60,000	

The offset to the $220,000 debit to Accumulated Depreciation is not shown because it is part of a compound entry showing the sale of the property. This transaction is illustrated in the next set of exercises.

Exercise A5-5 **Equipment and Accumulated Depreciation Account Relationships.** This exercise is more realistic and more challenging than the earlier truck example because it involves multiple assets and only some of the old items are sold during the year.

Dropit Express Company began the year with several delivery trucks. During the year, depreciation expense was $60,000. At the end of the year, Dropit sold trucks that originally cost $48,000 for a $15,000 gain on sale. Then the company bought new trucks. The following T-accounts show the beginning and ending balances for the Truck and Accumulated Depreciation accounts. How much did the company receive on the sale of the old trucks? What was the cost of the new trucks?

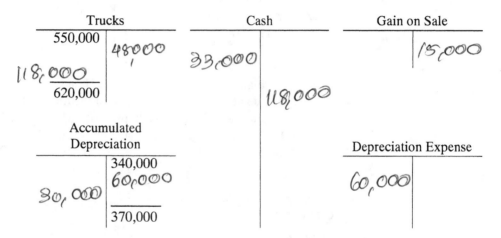

Solution The cash received from the sale of the old trucks was $33,000. Dropit bought new trucks for $118,000. First record the depreciation expense.

At this point, the beginning accumulated depreciation and the $60,000 resulting from the expense total $400,000. Since the ending balance is only $370,000, we know that the account was reduced by $30,000. The most likely reason is the removal of the depreciation accumulated on the trucks that were sold. Therefore, we know that the accumulated depreciation on the trucks that were sold was $30,000. This permits us to develop the following journal entry:

Cash	*?*	
Accumulated Depreciation	*30,000*	
Trucks		*48,000*
Gain on Sale		*15,000*

This tells us that the cash received on the sale must have been $33,000.

At this point, we can record the entries for depreciation and the sale in the T-accounts as follows:

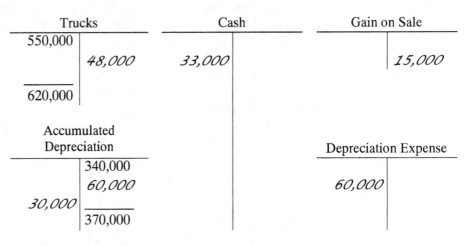

Trucks		Cash		Gain on Sale	
550,000					
	48,000	*33,000*			*15,000*
620,000					

Accumulated Depreciation			Depreciation Expense	
	340,000			
	60,000		*60,000*	
30,000				
	370,000			

Now we've explained everything except the Truck account. This account has a $502,000 balance after removing the cost of the old trucks that were sold. Since the ending balance is $620,000, we know that the company bought new trucks for $118,000. If you debit the Truck account for this amount, you'll have the correct ending balance.

Trucks		Cash		Gain on Sale	
550,000					
	48,000	33,000			15,000
118,000			*118,000*		
620,000					

Accumulated Depreciation			Depreciation Expense	
	340,000			
	60,000		60,000	
30,000				
	370,000			

Exercise A5-6

Plant and Equipment Account Relationships. This exercise incorporates the same concepts as the preceding one. The approach is the same, but the information that is given and the information to be determined differ.

Gregory Company's beginning and ending Equipment and Accumulated Depreciation account balances for the year are shown in the following T-accounts. During the year, the company bought equipment for $100,000. Depreciation expense for the year was $40,000. Also during the year, the company received $50,000 from the sale of old equipment. After recording the purchase and depreciation expense in the T-accounts, calculate the gain or loss on sale by completing the journal entry for the sale. Finally, show the various entries in Gregory's T-accounts.

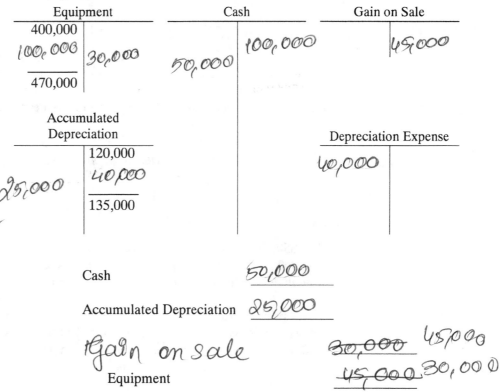

Equipment		Cash		Gain on Sale	
400,000					
100,000	30,000	50,000	100,000		45,000
470,000					

Accumulated Depreciation		Depreciation Expense	
	120,000	40,000	
25,000	40,000		
	135,000		

Cash   50,000

Accumulated Depreciation   25,000

Gain on sale   30,000   45,000
Equipment   45,000 30,000

Solution   The gain on sale must be $45,000. First record the purchase of new equipment and depreciation expense for the year. This prepares the books for the entry on sale of the old equipment.

Equipment	Cash	Gain on Sale
400,000		
100,000	*100,000*	
470,000		

Accumulated Depreciation		Depreciation Expense
120,000		
40,000		*40,000*
135,000		

Then the journal entry to show the sale of equipment is as follows:

Cash	*50,000*	
Accumulated Depreciation	*25,000*	
Equipment		*30,000*
Gain on Sale		*45,000*

The $50,000 selling price was given. We know that the old equipment cost $30,000 because the company had to adjust the Equipment account by this amount to obtain the $470,000 ending account balance.

Analysis of the Accumulated Depreciation account provides the $25,000 adjustment to that account resulting from the sale. This account increased by the $40,000 depreciation expense. Therefore, it must have been reduced by $25,000 to provide the ending account balance.

In solving for the gain on sale, one approach is to set credits equal to debits. Since the debits total $75,000, the gain on sale must be $45,000 to provide for equality. Another way to look at the situation is to start with the book value of the equipment that was sold. The journal entry shows this to be $5,000 ($30,000 cost less $25,000 accumulated depreciation). Comparing this to the $50,000 selling price provides the $45,000 gain.

Selling price	$50,000
Book value	5,000
Gain on sale	$45,000

The completed T-accounts show the following:

Equipment			Cash			Gain on Sale	
400,000				100,000			45,000
100,000							
	30,000		50,000				
470,000							

Accumulated Depreciation				Depreciation Expense	
	120,000			40,000	
	40,000				
25,000					
	135,000				

This is a fairly challenging problem. Congratulations if you're comfortable with it! If not, practice with the preceding exercises should prepare you to try this one again.

Inventory

You learned previously that the Inventory, Accounts Payable, and Cost of Goods Sold accounts are closely related. First companies purchase inventory on account and then they pay suppliers. Finally they sell the goods. Inventory increases with purchases and decreases with the cost of goods sold. Accounts payable increase with purchases and decrease when suppliers are paid. The next several exercises develop analysis skills with respect to the Inventory, Accounts Payable, and Cost of Goods Sold accounts.

Exercise A5-7

Inventory and the Cost of Goods Sold. Fry Company's cost of goods sold is $300,000. Using the beginning and ending account balances shown in the T-accounts, calculate the amount of inventory purchases.

Inventory		Accounts Payable		Cost of Goods Sold	
70,000					
280,000	*300,000*		*280,000*	*300,000*	
50,000					

Solution

Given the $300,000 cost of goods sold, inventory purchases are $280,000 as shown in the following accounts:

Inventory		Accounts Payable		Cost of Goods Sold	
70,000					
280,000			280,000		
	300,000			300,000	
50,000					

The first step is to record the $300,000 cost of goods sold and the reduction of inventory. This tells us that purchases, the addition to inventory total $280,000. Otherwise, ending inventory would not be $50,000.

Exercise A5-8

Inventory and Accounts Payable. In this exercise, the analyst works backward to calculate the cash paid for merchandise purchases. We know that the company first purchases inventory and then pays on account.

Partridge Corporation's purchases were $700,000. Using the beginning and ending account balances shown in the Accounts Payable T-account, calculate the amount paid on account. Remember that accounts payable increase with purchases and decrease with cash payments.

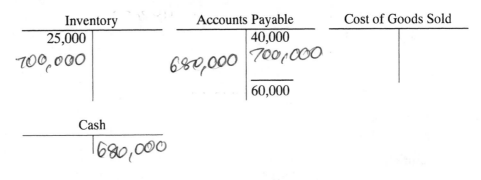

Solution

The amount paid on account was $680,000. Accounts payable increased by $700,000 when the company purchased inventory. Then payables must have been reduced by $680,000 to result in the $60,000 ending balance. In most cases, reductions in payables mean payments.

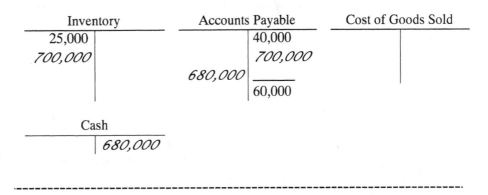

Exercise A5-9

Inventory, Accounts Payable, and the Cost of Goods Sold. Bridge Corporation's cost of goods sold was $400,000. Beginning and ending Inventory and Accounts Payable balances are as shown. How much cash was paid for purchases?

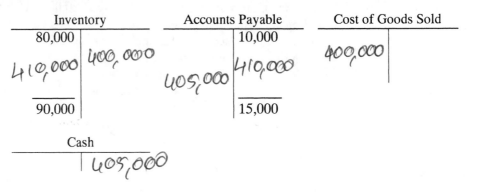

Solution

The analysis of accounts shows that cash payments were $405,000. Your first step should be to reduce inventory for the cost of goods sold. Then to explain the change in inventory, purchases must be $410,000. The T-accounts to this point are as follows:

Inventory		Accounts Payable		Cost of Goods Sold	
80,000			10,000		
	400,000			400,000	
410,000			410,000		
90,000			15,000		

Cash

We know that payments for inventory reduce Accounts Payable. Given the beginning and ending balances for Accounts Payable and the $410,000 addition, payments must have been $405,000.

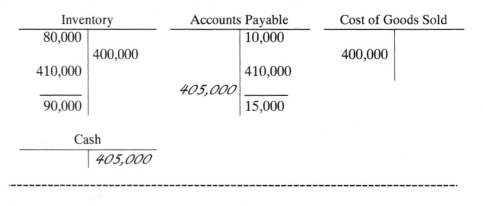

Exercise A5-10   **Inventory, Accounts Payable, and the Cost of Goods Sold.** Beginning and ending Inventory and Accounts Payable balances are shown in the following T-accounts. The beginning cash balance is also shown. During the year, purchases were $100,000 and payments for these purchases were $95,000. Calculate the cost of goods sold and the ending cash balance.

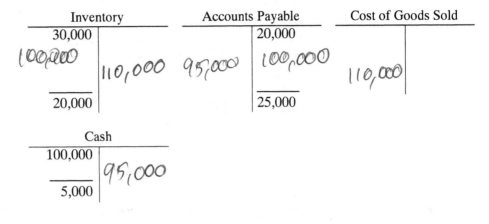

Solution   The cost of goods sold is $110,000 and the ending cash balance is $5,000. As shown in the following T-accounts, inventory increases with purchases and decreases with the cost of goods sold. Similarly, payables increase with purchases on account and decrease with payments to suppliers.

The accounts show the $100,000 increase in inventory and accounts payable resulting from the purchases on account. The cost of goods sold has to be $110,000 to leave $20,000 as ending inventory. Similarly, the beginning cash balance was reduced by the $95,000 payment on account. This leaves $5,000 as the ending cash balance.

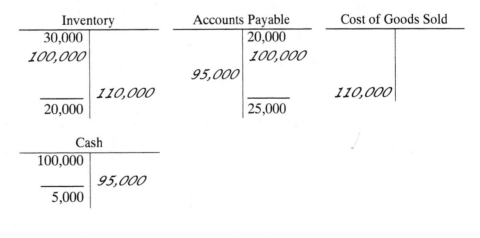

Chapter 6

Twenty questions
(Practice exercises)

This chapter consists entirely of review exercises. Comfort with this material indicates a solid understanding of the accounting system. It isn't necessary to work all practice exercises correctly on the first try. Review the appropriate chapters for missed material. Then work these exercises as often as necessary.

The exercises are divided into two parts. Direct method exercises that emphasize the mechanics of the accounting system come first. Indirect method problems are presented in the Appendix to Chapter 6 to help you develop skills in analysis and in estimating cash flows.

Exercise 6-1

Retained Earnings Warm-Up. Carolina Corporation begins the year with retained earnings of $100,000. During the year, the corporation earns $40,000 and declares dividends of $15,000.

Carolina Corporation
Change in retained earnings

Beginning Retained Earnings	$100,000
Add: Income	40,000
Less: Dividends Declared	— 15,000
Ending Retained Earnings	125,000

Carolina should report ending retained earnings of

a. $100,000.
b. $115,000.
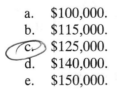
c. $125,000.
d. $140,000.
e. $150,000.

Solution C. Retained earnings increased by $25,000 to $125,000. We know that retained earnings increase with income ($40,000) and decrease with dividends ($15,000).

Carolina Corporation
Change in retained earnings

Beginning Retained Earnings	$100,000
Add: Income	40,000
Less: Dividends Declared	-15,000
Ending Retained Earnings	$125,000

Exercise 6-2 **Balance Sheet Relationships**. Portions of Home Company's balance sheet were damaged by spilled coffee. Using your knowledge of balance sheet relationships, calculate the ending Capital Stock account balance.

Home Company
Balance sheet at December 31, 20x5

Assets		Liabilities and Equity	
Cash	$ 40,000	Accounts Payable	$60,000
Inventory	100,000	Capital Stock	? *100,000*
Investments	100,000	Retained Earnings	80,000
	$240,000		$?
			240,000

Tip: Remember that assets equal liabilities plus owners' equity.

The balance in the Capital Stock account is

a. $80,000.
(b.) $100,000.
c. $120,000.
d. $150,000.
e. $180,000.

Solution B. Given that Assets = Liabilities + Owners' Equity, liabilities and owners' equity must equal the $240,000 balance of the assets. This means that the balance in the Capital Stock account must be $100,000.

Home Company
Balance sheet at December 31, 20x5

Assets		Liabilities and Equity	
Cash	$ 40,000	Accounts Payable	$ 60,000
Inventory	100,000	Capital Stock	100,000
Investments	100,000	Retained Earnings	80,000
	$240,000		$240,000

The next two exercises help you test your ability to classify balance sheet items as assets, liabilities, or owners' equity.

Exercise 6-3

Assets and Liabilities. All of Associated Company's balance sheet accounts except cash are shown here:

Associated Company
Balance sheet items at December 31, 20x3

Expenses Payable	$ 20,000
Retained Earnings	230,000
Inventory	10,000
Equipment	80,000
Capital Stock	110,000
Note Payable	40,000
Factory	230,000

Tip: Remember that assets represent value to the business, and liabilities are obligations.

For this exercise, first classify the accounts as assets, liabilities, or owners' equity. Then use the balance sheet equation to calculate the missing amounts.

Associated's cash balance is

a. $40,000.
b. $50,000.
c. $70,000.
d. $80,000.
e. $100,000.

Solution

D. The cash balance must be $80,000. Inventory, equipment, and the factory are assets. The remaining items reflect liabilities or owners' equity. Liabilities and owners' equity total $400,000. Therefore, since Assets = Liabilities + Equity, assets must also total $40,000. The cash balance is the amount necessary to provide $400,000 in total assets. After substituting for cash, the completed balance sheet shows the following:

Associated Company
Balance sheet at December 31, 20x3

Assets		Liabilities and Equity	
Cash	$ 80,000	Expenses Payable	$ 20,000
Inventory	10,000	Note Payable	40,000
Equipment	80,000	Capital Stock	110,000
Factory	230,000	Retained Earnings	230,000
	$400,000		$400,000

Exercise 6-4

Classifying Accounts. This exercise involves recognition of asset, liability, and owners' equity accounts. Hillside Company's balance sheet at the beginning of 20x6 shows the following:

Cash	$500
Capital Stock	100
Accounts Receivable	48
Accumulated Depreciation	90
Accounts Payable	30
Inventory	10
Retained Earnings	528
Equipment	190

Tip: Assets represent items of value to the business.

Hillside's assets (net of accumulated depreciation) on January 1, 20x6 total

  a. $621.
  b. $658.
  c. $660.
  d. $710.
  e. $719.

Solution

B. Hillside's total assets on January 1 are $658. The assets are cash, accounts receivable, inventory, and equipment. Accumulated Depreciation, a contra account, reduces the balance of total assets. All remaining accounts are liability or equity accounts. This is seen in the following complete balance sheet.

Hillside Company
Balance sheet at January 1, 20x6

Assets		Liabilities and Equity	
Cash	$500	Accounts Payable	$ 30
Accounts Receivable	48	Capital Stock	100
Inventory	10	Retained Earnings	528
Equipment	190		$658
Accumulated Depreciation	-90		
	$658		

Exercise 6-5

Transactions. Hillside Company examined in Exercise 6-4 begins 20x6 with the following balance sheet:

Hillside Company
Balance sheet at January 1, 20x6

Assets		Liabilities and Equity	
Cash	$500	Accounts Payable	$ 30
Accounts Receivable	48	Capital Stock	100
Inventory	10	Retained Earnings	528
Equipment	190		$658
Accumulated Depreciation	-90		
	$658		

This exercise involves recording transactions and adjusting entries. The challenge is to find the end-of-year total assets. It is not necessary to close the books for this determination.

1.	Cash Contributions by Shareholders	$ 40
2.	Inventory Purchased on Account	610
3.	Sales on Account	900
4.	Collections of Receivables	880
5.	Payments on Account	620
6.	Salary Expense (Payments $90)	100
7.	Dividends Declared (Paid $25)	30

Tip: Remember that Accumulated Depreciation is a contra account that offsets the Equipment account balance.

At the end of the year, Hillside uses the following information to make adjusting entries:

a.	Depreciation expense	$40
b.	Ending inventory	25

The following T-accounts should help you organize your work.

Cash

500	
40	
8 80	
	620
	90
	25
685	

Accounts Payable

	30
620	610
	20

Capital Stock

	100
	40
	140

Inventory

10	
610	595
25	

Salaries Payable

	100
90	
	10

Retained Earnings

	528

Accounts Receivable

48	
900	880
68	

Dividends Payable

	30
25	
	5

Sales Revenue

	900

Equipment

190	

Salary Expense

100	

Depreciation Expense

40	

Accumulated Depreciation

	90
	40
	130

Dividends Declared

30	

Cost of Goods Sold

595	

Hillside's assets (net of accumulated depreciation) on December 31, 19x6 total

a. $742.
b. $758.
c. $823.
d. $827.
e. $838.

Solution   E. Ending total assets sum to $838. Hillside's completed T-accounts and journal entries follow:

Cash			Accounts Payable			Capital Stock	
500				30			100
40			620	*610*			*40*
880				20			140
	620						
	90		Salaries Payable			Retained Earnings	
	25			100			528
685			90	—			
				10			

Inventory			Dividends Payable			Sales Revenue	
10				30			*900*
610	*595*		25	—			
25				5			

Accounts Receivable						Salary Expense	
48						*100*	
900	*880*						
68							

Equipment						Depreciation Expense	
190						*40*	

Accumulated Depreciation			Dividends Declared			Cost of Goods Sold	
	90		30			595	
	40						
	130						

The journal entries follow:

1. **Cash Contributions by Shareholders**

Cash	*40*	
Capital Stock		*40*

2. **Inventory Purchased on Account**

Inventory	*610*	
Accounts Payable		*610*

3. **Sales on Account**

Accounts Receivable	900	
Sales Revenue		900

4. **Collections of Receivables**

Cash	880	
Accounts Receivable		880

5. **Payments on Account**

Accounts Payable	620	
Cash		620

6. **Salary Expense $100 (Payments $90)**

Salary Expense	100	
Cash		90
Salaries Payable		10

7. **Dividends Declared (Paid $25)**

Dividends Declared	30	
Cash		25
Dividends Payable		5

a. **Depreciation Expense $40**

Depreciation Expense	40	
Accumulated Depreciation		40

b. **Ending Inventory $25 ($595 Sold)**

Cost of Goods Sold	595	
Inventory		595

Exercise 6-6

Closing the Books. Now it's time for Hillside Company to close the books and determine ending retained earnings. Before closing, the account balances are as follows:

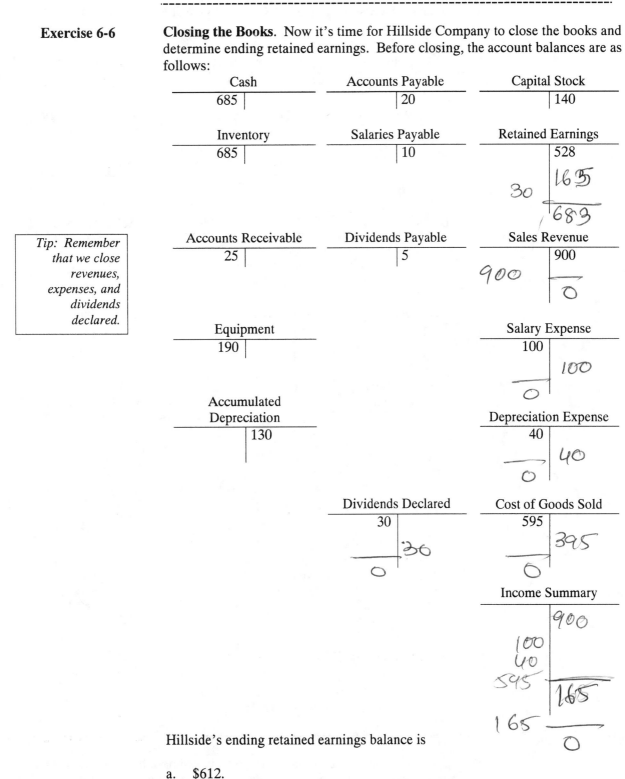

Cash		Accounts Payable		Capital Stock	
685			20		140

Inventory		Salaries Payable		Retained Earnings	
685			10		528
				30	165
					683

Tip: Remember that we close revenues, expenses, and dividends declared.

Accounts Receivable		Dividends Payable		Sales Revenue	
25			5		900
				900	0

Equipment				Salary Expense	
190				100	
					100
				0	

Accumulated Depreciation				Depreciation Expense	
	130			40	
					40
				0	

Dividends Declared		Cost of Goods Sold	
30		595	
	30		595
0		0	

Income Summary	
	900
100	
40	
595	165
165	
	0

Hillside's ending retained earnings balance is

a. $612.
b. $624.
c. $637.
d. $663.
e. $704.

Solution

E. Ending retained earnings are $663. Steps in the closing process are shown in the following T-accounts:

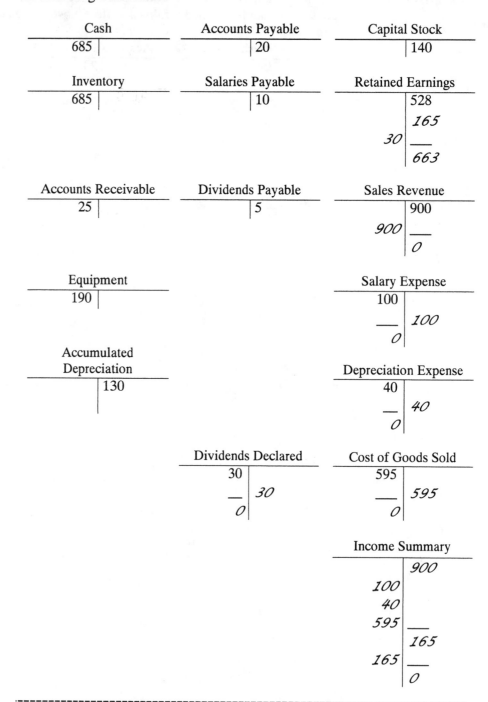

Cash		Accounts Payable		Capital Stock	
685			20		140

Inventory		Salaries Payable		Retained Earnings	
685			10		528
					165
				30	
					663

Accounts Receivable		Dividends Payable		Sales Revenue	
25			5		900
				900	
					0

Equipment				Salary Expense	
190				100	
				—	*100*
				0	

Accumulated Depreciation				Depreciation Expense	
	130			40	
				—	*40*
				0	

Dividends Declared		Cost of Goods Sold	
30		595	
—	*30*	—	*595*
0		*0*	

Income Summary	
	900
100	
40	
595	
	165
165	
	0

We could find retained earnings in this exercise without the closing entries. From the previous exercise, the assets are $838 and liabilities total $35. Thus, owners' equity is $803. Since we know that capital stock is $140, retained earnings must be $663. One advantage of closing entries is that they help ensure that income reconciles with the balance sheet items. You can refer to Chapters 2, 3, and 4 for help with these concepts.

Exercise 6-7

Interest Receivable. At the beginning of the year, Rutherford Corporation's Interest Receivable account balance is $9,000. During the year, the company earned $100,000 in interest and collected $102,000. T-accounts are provided to help you find the ending Interest Receivable account balance.

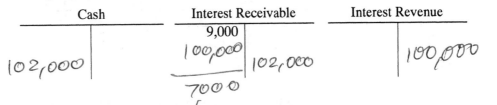

Cash	Interest Receivable	Interest Revenue
	9,000	
102,000	100,000 102,000	100,000
	7000	

The ending Interest Receivable account balance is

a. $5,000.
b. $7,000.
c. $9,000.
d. $11,000.
e. $13,000.

Solution

B. The ending receivable is $7,000. First we increase interest receivable by $100,000 to reflect revenue. Then we reduce the receivable by $102,000, the amount collected.

Cash	Interest Receivable	Interest Revenue
	9,000	
	100,000	100,000
102,000	_____ 102,000	
	7,000	

Exercise 6-8

Prepaid Accounts. Jones Corporation begins the year with $2,000 in prepaid insurance. During the year, Jones pays $21,000 for insurance. Insurance expense during the year is $22,000. The relevant T-accounts are as follows:

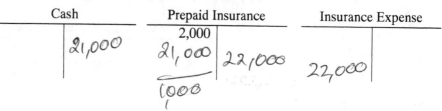

Cash	Prepaid Insurance	Insurance Expense
21,000	2,000	22,000
	21,000 22,000	
	(1000)	

The ending Prepaid Insurance account balance is

Tip: *Remember that prepaid accounts increase with payments and decrease with expenses.*

a. $1,000.
b. $2,000.
c. $3,000.
d. $4,000.
e. $5,000.

Solution

A. The ending Prepaid Insurance account balance is $1,000. This account increases by the $21,000 payment and decreases by the $22,000 expense as shown in the following entries.

Cash	Prepaid Insurance	Insurance Expense
21,000	2,000	22,000
	21,000 22,000	
	1,000	

Exercise 6-9

Accounting for Depreciable Property. Federal Group buys new recording equipment for $60,000. The business expects to use the equipment for four years and then sell it for $20,000.

At the end of <u>two</u> years, the Accumulated Depreciation account balance will be

Tip: Remember that each year's depreciation <u>accumulates</u> in the Accumulated Depreciation account.

a. $0.
b. $10,000.
c. $15,000.
d. $20,000.
e. $23,000.

Solution

D. Accumulated depreciation will be $20,000 at the end of two years. The annual depreciation is:

Annual depreciation expense   = Amount to be depreciated / Expected life

= (Cost-Residual value) / Expected life

= ($60,000 - $20,000) / 4 years

= $10,000 per year

After two years, accumulated depreciation will be $20,000.

You can review Chapter 5 for help with plant and equipment accounts.

Exercise 6-10   **Accounting for Depreciable Property.** Federal Group buys new recording equipment for $60,000 and expects to use it for four years and then sell it for $20,000. Previously, we determined that depreciation is $10,000 per year. At the end of <u>three</u> years, Federal actually sells the equipment for $5,000. Complete the T-accounts just prior to sale:

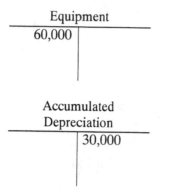

Equipment
| 60,000 | |

Accumulated Depreciation
| | 30,000 |

Then find the gain or loss on sale.

Selling price	5,000
Book value	30,000
Gain on sale	25,000

Finally, record the journal entry to be sure it is a loss rather than a gain.

Cash	5,000
Loss on Sale	25,000
~~Or Gain on Sale~~	
Equipment	30,000

The gain or loss on sale is

a. $25,000 loss.
b. $10,000 loss.
c. $No gain or loss.
d. $10,000 gain.
e. $25,000 gain.

(answer a. is circled)

Solution   A. Federal Group reports a $25,000 loss on sale. At the end of three years, accumulated depreciation is $30,000 ($10,000 per year). Subtracting this amount from the $60,000 cost results in a $30,000 book value. Since the selling price is only $5,000, the loss is $25,000. Just prior to sale, the T-accounts show the following:

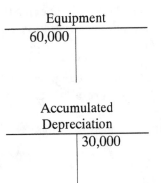

Equipment	
60,000	

Accumulated Depreciation	
	30,000

The loss on sale is as follows:

Selling price	$ 5,000
Book value	30,000
Loss on sale	$25,000

Finally, the journal entry to record the sale is as follows:

Cash	5,000	
Loss on Sale	25,000	
Equipment, Net		30,000

Appendix to Chapter 6
exercises in financial analysis

Exercise A6-1

Retained Earnings. Dalmatian Corporation begins the year with $200,000 of retained earnings. During the year, the corporation earns $60,000. Ending retained earnings are $220,000.

Dalmatian Corporation
Change in retained earnings

Beginning Retained Earnings	$200,000
Add: Income	*60,000*
Less: Dividends Declared	*- 40,000*
Ending Retained Earnings	$220,000

The corporation declared the following dividends to Sandra, Sally, and Susie, the three shareholders:

a. $20,000
b. $40,000
c. $60,000
d. $80,000
e. $90,000

Solution

B. Retained earnings increased by $20,000. Since income was $60,000, dividends must have been $40,000.

Dalmatian Corporation
Change in retained earnings

Beginning Retained Earnings	$200,000
Add: Income	60,000
Less: Dividends Declared	-40,000
Ending Retained Earnings	$220,000

Exercise A6-2   **Retained Earnings**. Frigid Corporation begins the year with retained earnings of $300,000. During the year, the company reports income. It then declares dividends of $30,000. Ending retained earnings are $310,000.

Frigid Corporation
Change in retained earnings

Beginning Retained Earnings	$300,000
Add: Income	*40,000*
Less: Dividends Declared	*−30,000*
Ending Retained Earnings	$310,000

Income is for the year is

a. $10,000.
b. $25,000.
c. $30,000.
d. $40,000.
e. $50,000.

Solution   D. Retained earnings increased by $10,000. Dividends reduced retained earnings by $30,000. Therefore, income must have been $40,000.

Frigid Corporation
Change in retained earnings

Beginning Retained Earnings	$300,000
Add: Income	40,000
Less: Dividends Declared	-30,000
Ending Retained Earnings	$310,000

Exercise A6-3

Retained Earnings. Conrad Corporation begins the year with retained earnings of $500,000. During the year, the company produces more product than it can sell and reports a loss. Conrad then declares dividends of $20,000. Ending retained earnings are $470,000.

Conrad Corporation
Change in retained earnings

Beginning Retained Earnings	$500,000
Less: Loss	*−10,000*
Less: Dividends Declared	*− 20,000*
Ending Retained Earnings	$470,000

Conrad Corporation's loss for the year is

  a. $5,000.
  b. $7,000.
  c. $9,000.
  d. $10,000.
  e. $15,000.

Solution

D. The loss was $10,000. Since dividends reduced retained earnings by $20,000, the loss had to be $10,000 for retained earnings to fall by $30,000.

Conrad Corporation
Change in retained earnings

Beginning Retained Earnings	$500,000
Less: Loss	-10,000
Less: Dividends Declared	-20,000
Ending Retained Earnings	$470,000

Exercise A6-4

Basic Asset, Liability, Equity Relationships. Future Corporation began business in early 20x4. Investors paid $60,000 for shares of capital stock early in the year. No additional shares were issued during the year. At the end of the year, net assets (assets less liabilities) are $90,000. Dividends of $20,000 were declared and paid during 20x4.

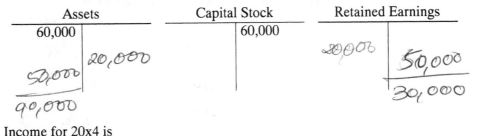

Assets		Capital Stock		Retained Earnings	
60,000			60,000		
	20,000			20,000	
50,000					50,000
90,000					30,000

Income for 20x4 is

a.	$5,000.
b.	$20,000.
c.	$30,000.
d.	$40,000.
e.	$50,000.

> *Tip: Ending owners' equity is given. The Capital Stock and Retained Earnings accounts both changed.*

Solution

E. Owners' equity (net assets) is given as $90,000 at the end of the year. We know that owners' equity has two main components, capital stock and retained earnings. Since capital stock is $60,000, retained earnings must be $30,000. We also know that dividends were $20,000. This means that retained earnings first increased by $50,000 and then decreased by $20,000 to end at $30,000 after dividends. The $50,000 increase is income. This is shown in the following accounts:

Assets		Capital Stock		Retained Earnings	
60,000			60,000		
	20,000			20,000	
50,000					50,000
90,000					30,000

The key to this exercise is knowing that owners' equity consists of capital stock and retained earnings. Generally, capital stock changes only when the company receives additional funds from investors in exchange for shares. Except in unusual circumstances, retained earnings change only as a result of income (or loss) and dividends.

Exercise A6-5

Basic Asset, Liability, Equity Relationships with Losses. At the beginning of the year, Peterson Company's capital stock was $100,000 and retained earnings were $20,000. The business does not have any liabilities. Ending assets are $128,000. During the year, shareholders invested an additional $25,000 in capital stock. Dividends declared and paid during the year were $10,000.

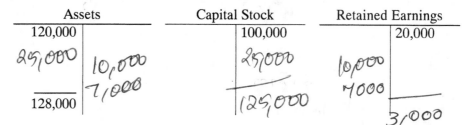

Peterson's loss for the year is

a. $5,000.
b. $6,000.
c. $7,000.
d. $8,000.
e. $10,000.

Solution

C. The loss is $7,000. First, calculate the ending Capital Stock account balance ($100,000 plus $25,000) Then, with ending assets given as $128,000, we know that ending retained earnings are only $3,000. How could retained earnings fall to only $3,000? The beginning balance was $20,000. Dividends reduced this to $10,000. Then a loss must have caused the additional reduction to $3,000. This is shown as follows:

Assets		Capital Stock		Retained Earnings	
120,000			100,000		20,000
25,000			25,000		
	10,000			10,000	
	7,000			7,000	
128,000			125,000		3,000

Please refer to Chapter 1 for more practice with these concepts.

Exercise A6-6

Interest Receivable. Mallard Corporation began the year with $8,000 of interest receivable and ended the year with interest receivable of $5,000. During the year, the company earned $80,000 of interest revenue.

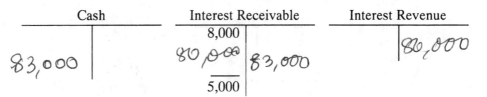

Cash	Interest Receivable	Interest Revenue
83,000	8,000	80,000
	80,000	83,000	
	5,000	

The cash collected from borrowers was

a. $77,000.
b. $79,000.
c. $80,000.
d. $81,000.
e. $83,000.

Tip: The treatment of interest receivable is basically the same as for accounts receivable.

Solution

E. Cash collections were $83,000. First record the $80,000 revenue and increase in receivables. Collections had to be $83,000 to provide the $5,000 ending cash balance.

Cash	Interest Receivable	Interest Revenue
	8,000	
	80,000	80,000
83,000		83,000	
	5,000	

Review Chapter 4 for help with receivables and payables.

Exercise A6-7

Prepaid Accounts. Commerce Corporation begins the year with $12,000 in prepaid rent and ends the year with $15,000 of prepaid rent. During the year, rent expense is $200,000. The relevant T-accounts are as follows:

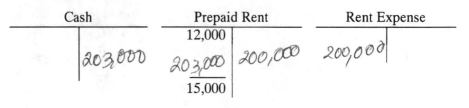

Tip: Remember that prepaid rent increases with rent payments and decreases with rent expense

The amount paid to the landlord during the year was

a. $197,000.
b. $199,000.
c. $200,000.
d. $201,000.
e. $203,000.

Solution

E. Commerce Corporation paid the landlord $203,000. The $200,000 rent expense reduces prepaid rent. Therefore, prepaid rent must be increased by $203,000 to provide the $15,000 ending balance. Prepaid rent increases when cash is paid to the landlord. The transactions are shown in the following T-accounts:

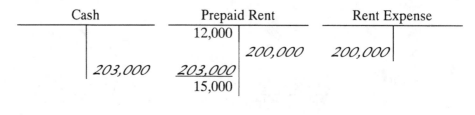

Prepaid accounts were covered in Chapter 5.

Exercise A6-8

Plant and Equipment Accounts. At the beginning of the year, Street Company's account balances for Equipment and Accumulated Depreciation were $300,000 and $100,000, respectively. By year-end, the balances had increased to $400,000 and $151,000. Depreciation expense for the year was $70,000. The company paid $150,000 for new equipment and sold old equipment at a $25,000 loss. Your mission is to determine the selling price of the old equipment.

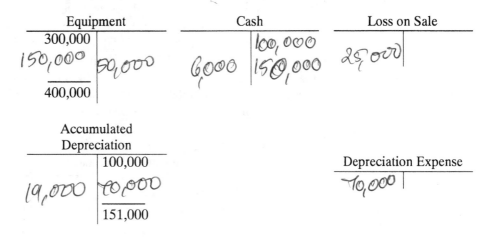

The old equipment's selling price is

   a. $2,000.
   b. $4,000.
   c. $6,000.
   d. $8,000.
   e. $10,000.

Solution

C. The selling price is $6,000. Just prior to the sale, after entering depreciation expense and the purchase of new equipment, the relevant accounts appear as follows:

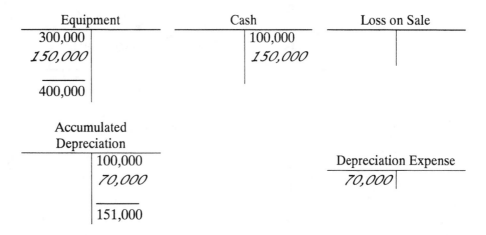

The following journal entry records the sale:

Cash	*6,000*	
Accumulated Depreciation	*19,000*	
Loss on Sale	*25,000*	
Equipment		*50,000*

Balances in both the Equipment and Accumulated Depreciation accounts can be determined from our knowledge of factors that cause changes in these accounts. The cost of equipment sold had to be $50,000 since this is the most straightforward explanation of the change in the Equipment account balance. Similarly, accumulated depreciation on the item sold had to be $19,000 to explain the ending Accumulated Depreciation account balance. This means that the book value of the items sold was $31,000.

Since the loss on sale is given, the cash received must have been $6,000. Now that we know the amount, we can confirm that $6,000 was received.

Selling price	$ 6,000
Book value	31,000
Loss on Sale	$25,000

After recording the equipment sale, the T-accounts appear as follows:

Equipment		Cash		Loss on Sale
300,000		100,000		
150,000		150,000		*25,000*
_____	*50,000*	*6,000*		
400,000				

Accumulated Depreciation		Depreciation Expense
	100,000	70,000
	70,000	
19,000	_____	
	151,000	

Exercise A6-9

Inventory, Accounts Payable, and the Cost of Goods Sold. The beginning and ending balances for the Inventory account were $20,000 and $24,000. For the Accounts Payable account, the beginning and ending balances were $5,000 and $4,000, respectively. During the year, the cost of goods sold was $100,000.

> *Tip: We know that inventories increase with purchases and decreases with the cost of goods sold.*

> *Tip: We also know that accounts payable increase with purchases and decrease with payments.*

Inventory	Accounts Payable	Cost of Goods Sold
20,000	5,000	
104,000 100,000	105,000 104,000	100,000
24,000	4,000	

Cash
105,000

The cash paid for inventory was

a. $96,000.
b. $100,000.
c. $101,000.
d. $104,000.
e. $105,000.

Solution

E. The cash paid for inventory was $105,000. We know that the cost of goods sold reduced inventory by $100,000. This means that the company purchased inventory for $104,000. Otherwise, the ending Inventory account balance would not be the amount shown. Since inventory purchases were $104,000, accounts payable must have also increased by this amount. Then payments had to be $105,000 to result in the $4,000 ending amount for Accounts Payable.

Inventory	Accounts Payable	Cost of Goods Sold
20,000	5,000	
104,000	104,000	
100,000	105,000	100,000
24,000	4,000	

Cash
105,000

Inventory, accounts payable, and cost of goods sold relationships were covered in Chapter 5.

Exercise A6-10

Dividends Payable. During the year, Bradley Company declared $30,000 in dividends. Beginning and ending Dividend Payable account balances were $5,000 and $5,500, respectively.

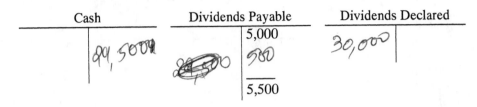

The dividend payments (cash) during the year were

a. $28,000.
b. $28,500.
c. $29,000.
d. $29,500.
e. $30,000.

> *Tip: Remember that the Dividends Payable account increases when dividends are declared. The account decreases when dividends are paid.*

Solution

D. Dividend payments were $29,500. Dividends payable increase by the amount of dividends declared and decrease with cash payments. Bradley Company's dividends declared were $30,000, and the payable increased by $500. This means that payments were only $29,500. The following T-accounts show the dividend declaration and payment as a compound entry:

Cash	Dividends Payable	Dividends Declared
	5,000	
29,500	*500*	*30,000*
	5,500	

The solution with two single entries leads to the same conclusion.

Cash	Dividends Payable	Dividends Declared
	5,000	
	30,000	*30,000*
29,500	29,500	
	5,500	